WHY PROPERTY WHY NOW

HOW TO INVEST IN PROPERTY AND BUY YOUR LIFE BACK

JOSH MASTERS

PUBLISHED BY

jericho publishing group

Published in Australia by
jericho publishing group

National Library of Australia
Cataloguing-in-Publication entry: A Cataloguing-in-Publication record is available from the
National Library of Australia.
Author: Josh Masters
Title: *Why Property Why Now*
Edition: Second
Publisher: jericho publishing group

ISBN 9780994422309 Pbk
ISBN 9780994422316 ePub
ISBN 9780994422323 Pbk

Includes index

Subjects: Property Investment, Real Estate, Business, Wealth Creation

Dewey Number

Editor: Susie Stevens, www.bold-type.com.au
Book design and typesetting: H2M Creative Services, www.h2m.com.au
Indexer: Glenda Browne
Printed by: Lightning Source

Acknowledgments

Stapledon Nigel 2007, 'Long Term Housing Prices in Australia and Some Economic Perspectives', a dissertation, Australian School of Business, University of New South Wales.

Stapledon Nigel 2010, 'A History of Housing Prices in Australia 1880–2010', discussion paper, Australian School of Business, University of New South Wales.

Residex   Suburb Report; Bondi Beach, May 19 2012, www.residex.com.au

                Suburb Report; St Kilda, Jan 28 2013, www.residex.com.au

While not quoted in the book, the author would like to acknowledge Robert Thaler's work on behavourial finance and Warren Buffett's work on value investing.

For my beautiful wife Julie
and her unending support

CONTENTS

Part 3 – Making it happen

INTRODUCTION

Have you ever stopped to think about how frantic our lives have become? Between ever increasing work, social and family commitments, there's barely enough time to down the three espressos needed to keep pace with it all.

Slowly and surely 21st century living has started to resemble the classic clichés that show us running furiously on the treadmill of life – extremely busy but failing to get ahead. In the pursuit of a better life, we have failed to realise the one thing that it all relies upon – our time. Instead, we have become consumed by a time famine.

The lack of abundance of time was the source of inspiration for this book – how we would prefer to spend our time, how that can be achieved through the right investment strategy and how that strategy can be executed successfully to give us more time to do the things in life that we want to do.

My own journey began in property investment some 15 years ago. I had just completed university and had been working as a waiter in Sydney's Darling Harbour to pay for my university fees. While some of my friends struggled, I was lucky enough to make good tips, and the late nights at work kept my social life to a minimum. As a result, I managed to save $26,000 by the time I had finished my degree. In my mind, it was enough money to quench my thirst for overseas adventure for years to come.

Fortunately for me, my parents thought otherwise. It was a simple stroke of genius that my parents suggested I invest some of the money, and an even larger stroke that I listened to them. I had become a property investor by accident. It was this decision alone that changed the course of my life.

By default, I had become involved in an investment class that was one of the most effective long-term wealth-building strategies on earth. It was prior to the boom of the early 2000s, and, although my first investment was only a modest townhouse in coastal New South Wales, this property alone tripled in value in a 10-year period. It became the catalyst for a succession of investments to follow.

I worked hard through those years and drew on my equity to start businesses from hospitality to online marketing. Ironically, through all of these years of entrepreneurial spirit, it was my passive, slow growing investment portfolio that was the quiet achiever. For very little effort on my part, my property portfolio far surpassed the profits that came from the blood, sweat and tears of any business venture I undertook.

At this point it's worth mentioning that I didn't grow up understanding the power of investing. I had a good head for numbers and a university education, but my understanding of moneymaking was that the harder you worked, the more you were paid. If you had a qualification, you were paid more, but you still had to work hard.

It's not until you experience the results of your growing financial wealth that you come to realise how it can change your life. To understand that you can own an asset that works for you – something that builds your wealth with little if any effort from you – can be a revelation.

And yet, it is a revelation that many of us fail to realise until it's too late.

In this increasingly frantic world, most of us are too busy to step back and think about how we would like to live our lives in the future, let alone pay for it. We may have dreams of making a million dollars, moving to the south of France or retiring at 40. But let's face it, unless we have a plan, those dreams can quickly pass by and leave us with a life that wasn't quite what we had hoped for. We are left working increasingly long hours with little time to think about the future until we actually arrive to find we simply didn't do enough to make our dreams a reality.

For those looking for a solution, it doesn't get easier. In a world of endless information, many of us come up against a multitude of complex investment ideas and detailed strategies only to walk out the other end more uncertain than when we began. As a result, we end up investing by default, led down the path by the most convincing sales person we encounter, uncertain of the purchase we've made and unsure about how to move forward in the future.

Add to this the fact that many of us will transact only two or three properties in our lifetime – barely enough to garner any experience or really understand how the market works. The situation leaves most of us exposed to any number of misjudgments and costly errors that may not be realised until many years later.

The whole situation leaves us with more questions than reassuring answers. Are we doing it right? Are we doing enough? How much is enough? Will my investments provide for the future?

Why Property Why Now aims to change that. Divided into three parts – Finding your reason; Creating your strategy; Making it happen – this book outlines the processes to follow to set and achieve successful financial goals.

The first part, 'Finding your reason', discards the notion of chasing financial goals for their own sake. Rather, this book looks at the concept of your time – how you want to spend this precious but finite resource and how time can work to achieve the financial goals that will allow you to live your life well.

The second part looks at property investment strategy, breaking your options down into a structure that is both understandable and easy to apply. This section investigates the most effective strategies for your situation so you end up with a property portfolio that outperforms the market without breaking the bank.

'Making it happen', the third part, outlines the most efficient and effective way to go through the buying process. Drawing on years of experience in buying property, it is the industry insider's notebook on what to do and what not to do to secure the best deal possible. It will walk you through the essential buying process, from securing finance to dealing with agents and the art of negotiation.

Delayed gratification

While this book is about capitalising on how you would prefer to spend your time, it is also about how to use time to build a property portfolio in a steady and sustainable way.

Be aware that building an investment portfolio requires just that – an investment of your time and resources now – so that you can reap benefits tomorrow.

While the strategies are not highly complex or advanced, they require some sacrifice before they bear fruit. If you can understand that you may have to make some adjustments today to get what you really want tomorrow, you will be miles ahead of most who don't have the fortitude to think past the next pay packet.

An umbrella disclaimer

The investment advice in this book is written at a general level. Throughout the book I recommend you get specific advice for your circumstances as your situation may mean you have to approach things differently. I can't stress enough how important it is to have the right team behind you to help you with these decisions. They will make choices for you that will affect the wellbeing of yourself and your loved ones, so choose carefully and be aware of their importance.

Some of the strategies that you find in this book may not work for you. You may find you have had a different experience or, because of your personal situation, you have had a different outcome. That's OK. There is no right or wrong way of doing things. This book focuses on saving time and building an ample portfolio of properties. If you find a quicker or better way of doing something, great. I would love to hear from you. You will find my details at the back of this book.

PART 1

FINDING YOUR REASON

TIME IS THE
NEW CURRENCY

*Time is the most valuable thing
a man can spend.*

Theophrastus

I shouldered my way through the door to the bar, shaking the rain off my suit jacket that I had been using as an umbrella only moments before. I looked around the room and found my friend Paul minding a table against the wall, already holding a beer in hand. Moments later I had ordered a drink myself and sat across from him, happy to be here after a hectic day of work.

'Nice of you to make it', he said. 'How's things?'

'Busy. Real busy', I said, as if a sign of success was measured by how frantic I was.

'We've been working on the new website for the business day and night and it finally went live last month. Suppliers are starting to come on board and it looks like we're going to be signing up a few contracts very soon. It's looking pretty good'.

'And Julie?'

'She's good, mate. We went back to the UK for Christmas and stopped in Dubai, Israel and India on the way. Great fun but I felt like needed a holiday from the holiday once we arrived back home.'

We both laughed. It had been a running joke between my fiancée and I that the most relaxing part of our holidays was in the air. Headphones on, phone and email off, nothing more to do but work out which movie to watch first.

Paul's life was as hectic but in a different way, and, after only two beers he had to go. 'Got to go. Leanne's looking after the bub and I want to get home before she goes to sleep.'

'Serious?' I said, not quite understanding what the fuss was all about.

'Absolutely. Kids are awesome mate. I spend my whole day waiting to get home just so I can see them. Don't worry, you'll understand one day'.

I'm sure I would, I thought. Right now I couldn't imagine where I would fit kids into my life. Julie was looking to expand her business into the States, while I was about to rush headlong into mine. Something would have to give.

'How about we catch up soon for dinner?' Paul asked.

'We're busy for the next three weeks. How are you looking in March?' I asked.

After flipping through his calendar Paul replied. 'Mate, we can do the 9th or the 23rd. Our babysitter is only good for Fridays'.

'No problem, how about I give you a call?' I said.

We left it at that, laughing and realising that it probably wouldn't be until my birthday in June that we would catch up again. We both rushed headlong out the door and into our busy lives.

Such stories are not uncommon. Work is consuming, time with friends all too fleeting and family responsibilities force us to trade one task for another. What has become of our lives?

Spending your time

Throughout the last century, it was believed that the more you worked, the more you could improve the quality of your life. The resourcefulness of western society meant that those who wished to get ahead could trade their time for an income to improve their lifestyle.

This is a fine concept until things start to get out of control. Trading an increasing amount of time for work can increase your income but leave very little time for other activities. 'All work and no play' means that time with friends and family becomes a thing of the past and the simplest pleasure of falling asleep with a book seems impossible.

Of course, you can choose to trade your time for more leisurely pursuits – reducing your time at work and your income – but living a more relaxed lifestyle.

Unfortunately, as soon as you reduce your income, you also reduce your choices. The less income, the fewer choices available to you. You're unable to take that holiday you wanted; you can't buy that car; you're unable to afford that house you want.

So where's the healthy balance? Does the pursuit of a better quality of life have to mean trading your time for either more income or more leisure?

The following activity is a simple exercise in understanding how you spend your time now between work and leisure.

Imagine you have two buckets – one represents work, the other leisure.

The more time you dedicate to your work bucket – through working longer hours or overtime – the more income you hope to receive. So the more time you can put into this bucket, generally the more your income will increase.

The other bucket is for time spent on leisure pursuits. The more time you spend relaxing with friends, eating out or travelling, the more income you spend. So the more time you put into this bucket, the more your income will generally decrease.

Using the two buckets above, estimate what percentage of time goes to filling the work bucket and what percentage goes in the leisure bucket.

Don't worry if it's not completely accurate. The idea is to get an understanding of the amount of time you currently dedicate in your waking hours to generating an income. Remember, this is a general exercise. It's not meant to be perfect.

The income trade

Even though you might enjoy work, you would undoubtedly prefer to be putting more time into your leisure bucket. So how do you fix this?

Most people will go through their whole lives taking out of one bucket to fill the other. Before long they realise that they need to put a little back in the other bucket because things aren't working out the way they'd hoped. This is what is known as work-life balance.

Those people who put too much of their time into their work bucket may end up with more money but little time for their leisure bucket. Others may put too much time into their leisure bucket, only to find that an emergency requires more of them financially than they're able to provide.

So how can you escape from this constant imbalance between work and leisure in a way that lets you build wealth and security but also lets you enjoy your life?

FLIPPING THE SYSTEM

Time is more valuable than money.
You can get more money,
but you cannot get more time.

Jim Rohn

Having a financial goal is vital if you're to create the life you want. Make no mistake how you spend your time will determine the quality of your life – not how much money you can earn.

A single-minded focus on your work bucket and making money will no doubt lead you to sacrificing the one thing that you set out to take control of in the first place – your time.

A businessman was at the pier of a small coastal Mexican village when a small boat with just one fisherman docked. Inside the small boat were several large yellowfin tuna. The businessman complimented the Mexican on the quality of his fish and asked how long it took to catch them. The Mexican replied only a little while. The businessman then asked why he didn't stay out longer and catch more fish? The Mexican said he had enough to support his family's immediate needs. The businessman then asked, but what do you do with the rest of your time? The Mexican fisherman said, 'I sleep late, fish a little, play with my children, take a siesta with my wife, Maria, stroll into the village each evening where I sip wine and play guitar with my amigos; I have a full and busy life.'

The businessman scoffed, 'I am a Harvard MBA and I could help you. You should spend more time fishing and with the proceeds buy a bigger boat. With the proceeds from the bigger boat you could buy several boats. Eventually you would have a fleet of fishing boats. Instead of selling your catch to a middleman, you would sell directly to the processor and eventually open your own cannery. You would control the product, processing and distribution. You would need to leave this small coastal fishing village and move to Mexico City, then LA and eventually New York City where you would run your expanding enterprise.'

The Mexican fisherman asked, 'But señor, how long will this all take?' To which the businessman replied, '15–20 years'. 'But what then, señor?'

The businessman laughed and said, 'That's the best part! When the time is right you would announce an IPO and sell your company stock to the public and become very rich. You would make millions.' 'Millions, señor? Then what?'

The businessman said, 'Then you would retire. Move to a small coastal fishing village where you would sleep late, fish a little, play with your kids, take a siesta with your wife, stroll to the village in the evenings where you could sip wine and play your guitar with your amigos.' The fisherman, smiling, looked up and said, 'Isn't that what I'm doing now?'

Author unknown

Unlike the fisherman in the village, your ideal life may require a little more income than you can bring in from selling a few fish. You may want to eat out at nice restaurants, have a holiday home or a boat that you can sail on the weekends. You may wish for the most lavish life possible, or one of simplicity and humbleness. In either case, all these things require an income. Even a humble fisherman needs to go to market to sell his fish so his family can survive.

The key is to recognise that the ideal life is defined by how to spend your time, not by how much income you generate. We've been conditioned to look toward our financial goals first, leaving us with the decision of how we're going to spend our time as an afterthought. Our life outside work becomes secondary. We strive to earn more and more with the vague notion that we're doing it to improve our standard of living and for our future, with little thought as to how we want that future to look. Financially we may be in superb shape, but when it comes to the quality of our lives, we're just treading water.

Time first, income second

This is what is called 'flipping the system'. It's about first deciding where you want to spend your time, then looking at the income you need to make that a reality.

This moves your focus away from the traditional goals of 'what' you want and towards what's really important to you. It allows you to create a life based on your values rather than the financial constraints that many tend to focus on. When you flip the system, you shift your thinking towards 'life' as the primary objective rather than 'work' as the goal.

In the next exercise, write five things you would like to add to your leisure bucket. What do you want to do in your leisure time? How would you spend it? Who would you spend it with? Dream big and forget any notion of what you're doing today or what you think it might cost. Imagine what your life could be like if anything were possible.

For example, you may wish to live in an apartment on the French Riviera with your own boat and mooring, doing nothing but sailing and drinking wine in the sun, or you may want to spend your time with your partner in a cottage in the Australian countryside watching your kids grow up. Take the next five minutes to write what you want out of life. This could be the best five minutes you've spent for a long time.

FIVE THINGS FOR MY LEISURE BUCKET

1. _____

2. _____

3. _____

4. _____

5. _____

If you've made some effort to complete this, congratulations! You're one of the few people who have made a conscious choice as to where you want to spend your time.

Most people will go their whole lives constantly reacting to what the world has brought them with little regard as to where they could have gone or what they could have created – they are 'living by default'. By defining where you want to spend your time, you have done what most people never do, and that is to create a life with intention.

The following chapter will look at how you can stop trading your own time for money. It will introduce the concept of replacing yourself in the system so that you can devote as much time as you choose to your leisure bucket and start living the life you've dreamed of.

REPLACING YOU

There is only one success – to be able to spend
your life in your own way.

Christopher Morley

Now that you have outlined where you would like to spend your time, you're going to think about how much income you need to 'replace you' in the income-earning system. Your goal will be to generate enough wealth so that you have no need to put any time into your work bucket unless you really want to. Wouldn't it be a great feeling to be able to make that choice, to spend as much time as you like adding to your leisure bucket and where any income from work was a bonus?

Look back over your leisure list and how you want to spend that time. How much do you think this lifestyle will cost you on a weekly basis? Again, there is no right or wrong answer here. The important thing is that you come up with a figure that's your best guess and that gives you a target to work towards.

Once you have a figure, write it down.

MY INCOME TARGET

$_____ per week

Well done! You have just worked out how much income you need to generate to live your ideal lifestyle – to replace yourself in the system – without having to put any more time into your work bucket. You now have a target that you can aim for and work towards that will give you the freedom to choose to work, rather than have to work.

Planning for success

To achieve that figure, you are going to need a plan. It's nice to have a goal to work towards but, unless you have a plan or some way of being able to achieve that goal, you might as well be daydreaming.

The problem is that, beyond winning the lotto or becoming an Internet sensation, like most of us, you are limited to the time you put in your work bucket to generate an income.

But what if you could create another bucket that produces income without requiring your time to earn income? What if you could create a third bucket to generate your wealth? In essence, this is the idea behind owning an asset.

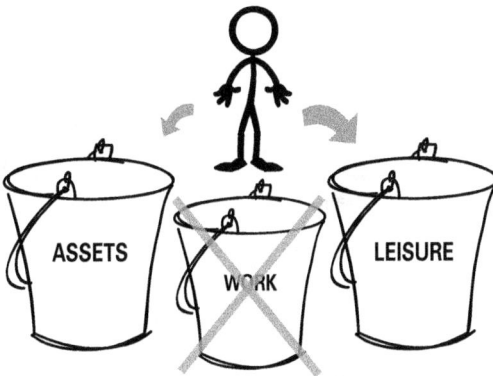

BENEFITS OF AN ASSET BUCKET

The distinguishing factor between the rich and the poor is not that the rich have more time to work to create more income. In many cases, they work less and, although they may be paid more for their actual time spent at work, the distinguishing factor that allows them to live the lifestyles they choose is that they have replaced themselves in the system – they have invested in their asset buckets that in turn creates wealth independently of the time they have available to them. This allows them to dedicate more of their time to their leisure bucket.

Not all assets are created equal

There are typically two different types of assets – appreciating assets and depreciating assets.

An appreciating asset, such as property, can continue to grow in value over time. A depreciating asset, such as a car, will tend to fall in value the moment you drive it away from the sales lot. These are both assets as they both hold value – both will put money in your pocket if you were to sell them.

For the moment, let's ignore the usual terms of appreciating and depreciating assets and take a look at assets from a different perspective.

Let's distinguish assets as:

- passive assets
- reactive assets
- active assets.

A passive asset may be a home cinema system or your sports equipment. It may be worth money if you were to sell it but it doesn't contribute to any direct form of income generation.

A reactive asset may be a tractor or a printing machine. This may be a depreciating asset but it is also an asset that, when operated, can directly generate income for the owner. An important distinction with this kind of asset, however, is that it is dependent on the owner to work. If the owner became sick or took a vacation, that asset would sit idle and would do nothing but gather dust.

An active asset is one that generates direct income for the owner and does so independently of whether the owner is present or not. A good example of this might be a government bond. When a government bond is purchased, it may yield 3.5% per year in income over its lifetime. The income is generated without the owner having to lift a finger for that asset to continue to build income.

This is the kind of asset that will build wealth while you lounge by the pool filling up your leisure bucket with mojitos. This is the kind of asset you'll like.

Property – the great active asset

Next to shares and cash, property is one of the biggest asset classes on earth. Throughout history it has acted as a source of wealth for those fortunate enough to own it and, to this day, regardless of the amount of wealth, most people prefer to convert their holdings into the safe and stable asset that property is known for.

Property really is one of the strongest active assets in the investment world. When utilised properly, it has the ability to bring true wealth and financial security to your household so that you can step away from the grind that is so often associated with work and devote your time to delivering your talents to the world in any way you see fit. From the creation of an entrepreneurial idea to walking your kids to school, make property work for you and the choice will be yours.

Let's quickly discover some of the characteristics that make property an ideal active asset to invest in, over and above alternative investments:

- leverage
- compound growth
- capital growth
- no margin calls
- low volatility.

Leverage

This is by far one of the strongest advantages available to property investors. Leverage is the ability to multiply your investment efforts with a relatively small outlay. For example, by investing only a small portion of your funds you can control an asset many times larger in value. When the value of that asset increases as little as 5% or 10%, this can often be equal to, or greater than, the initial amount you invested.

While this level of leverage can offer great returns, it is not without risk. However, lenders are usually happy to lend money for property purchases, not just because a home loan is a stable product that generates income, but also because the lending practice is considered quite safe. The money you borrow is being used to buy something quite tangible. You can see it, touch it, use it. It provides for one of the most basic needs on the planet, housing, and for that reason it will always hold value.

Compound growth

Compounding effectively means 're-investing the profits'. Albert Einstein was quoted as saying 'The most powerful force in the universe is compound interest'.

Let's say you invest $1,000, your 'principal amount', at an interest rate of 10% over the next 10 years. If you were to use a compounding investment, each year your 'winnings' would be put back into the account and re-invested for the next year.

At the end of 10 years, you will have accumulated $2,593, a total return of 159%. Even though the interest rate of your investment was consistently 10% over 10 years, your average rate of return over those 10 years was actually 15.9%. That's the magic of compounding growth.

So what's the difference between the compound growth experienced with property and that of a share portfolio or a savings account?

Unlike cash or shares that are quite liquid and can be traded in small parcels, property is treated as a single asset that can't generally be broken up or sold off based on the profits that are being generated.

If you make a profit on your share portfolio, you instantly have the ability to take those profits thereby reducing the compounding effect in the next phase of growth. As desirable as it might be to take these earnings, the nature of property as a single asset forces the owner to continue to compound profits.

You can see that while some regard this lack of flexibility as a disadvantage, for those investors who are willing to delay their profit taking, there is the potential for a much greater reward.

Capital growth

If you've ever listened to property experts talking about the historical growth levels in the property market, you will undoubtedly have heard them say that property values tend to double every seven to 10 years.

Here's an illustration to get a handle on how quickly it is assumed property will double in value.

PERCENTAGE GROWTH TO DOUBLE ASSET VALUE

10% growth per yr = **7 yrs** to double your asset (approx.)

7% growth per yr = **10 yrs** to double your asset (approx.)

THE RULE OF 72

To work out how long an investment takes to double its value is to use the Rule of 72 – divide 72 by the growth rate e.g. 72/7 = 10.2 years.

The most comprehensive study of Australian property prices to date has been that of Nigel Stapledon, who has analysed prices dating back as far as 1880.

Stapledon's studies have shown the property market experienced a steady price rise up until 1955 when property prices suddenly took off. From this point on, Australian property prices experienced an average of 8.6% increase per annum. This means, on average, the value of Australian property has doubled every 8.3 years for the past 50 years.

On average, the value of Australian property has doubled every 8.3 years for the past 50 years.

The effects of the global financial crisis (GFC) since 2007 have certainly seen markets lose their typical momentum, even with 50 years of data. Whatever the argument, it is clear that property has provided substantial gains over the last 50 years and stands as one of the more prominent asset classes available to invest in despite what may happen in the future.

No margin calls

As an investor in the share market, if you were to borrow $50,000 to boost the value of your share portfolio and the share value fell below its worth, alarm bells would likely ring for the lender. You then may be requested to sell to avoid any further losses to your (read 'their') principal amount, otherwise known as a 'margin call'.

Within the property market, however, the value of property at any given time is uncertain at best. This lack of clarity prevents lenders from tapping the investor on the shoulder to ask for their money back. Because the real value of the property is unknown, it can be determined only if the owner were to take the property to market.

The uncertain value of a property also prevents the owner 'checking in' to see how much they've made or lost, so they're more inclined to relax and let it run its course – which is exactly what's needed – as property investment requires a long-term commitment to reap significant rewards.

Low volatility

As an asset class, shares have been a much-loved darling of the Australian culture with around 43% of the adult population owning some sort of shares according to Canstar. However, the financial crisis of 2007 saw the value of shares plummet leaving the retirement funds of many investors in a dire situation.

The fact is, the share market is volatile. While massive profits can be achieved, history has shown that even the best-performing companies can be subject to dramatic downgrades and overnight declines that leave the shareholder with little option but to take a loss.

Property can be a much safer proposition because it is not subject to volatile swings – it neither falls dramatically nor rises to great heights on a day-to-day basis. While some investors may not have seen great gains in their property portfolios in the years since the GFC, the number would be in the minority.

As you can see, the basic principles of building wealth, such as leverage, compound growth and long-term stability, have all proven to be factors that have contributed to the advantages of property investment to build wealth over time.

Invest in property and you will be on the road to building your own asset bucket, eventually moving your time away from your work bucket to any area you see fit, leisure or otherwise.

The next chapter looks at exactly how much property you will need to replace the time you currently spend contributing to your work bucket and how you can create a portfolio to reach this future level of wealth.

STARTING WITH
THE END IN MIND

*If you don't know where you're going,
any road will get you there.*

Lewis Carroll, *Alice in Wonderland*

Now that property has been identified as an ideal active asset, creating a target that you can work toward is essential to your success. It will also act as a benchmark to show you're on the right track. Many people like the idea of property investment, but many fail to understand what results to expect. Subsequently, many people sell or give up before the asset has really had time to mature.

Planning your wealth creation

The key to success is to start with the end in mind, working backwards from a desired result to an outcome that you can start shooting for today.

To do this, you will need to:

- set a target
- adjust for inflation
- allow for growth.

Step 1: Set a target – how much do you want?

The following exercise will help you determine how much wealth you're aiming for. While a lot of people simply think in large sums of cash (I want one million dollars), think about building your target a little more strategically using your desired income level that you wrote down in the last chapter. This way you know that, by achieving this target, you will be able to spend your time as you choose.

To do this, take the income target that you wrote in the last chapter and write it under 'My target'. Then grab a calculator and follow the formula to work out your result. The example in the right-hand column shows how it works.

By starting with the desired weekly income figure and multiplying it by 52 weeks in the year, you end up with a figure that will be your yearly income. If you consider your gross rental yield as 5% less expenses of 1%, this allows you to calculate your end figure using a net yield of 4%.

WORK OUT YOUR INCOME TARGET

My target	Example
$_____ per wk	**$3000** per wk
× 52 weeks	× 52 weeks
= $_____ per yr	= **$156,000** per yr
÷ 0.04 (5% rental yield less 1% expenses)	÷ 0.04 (5% rental yield less 1% expenses)
= $_____	= **$3,900,000**

If you've done this task, congratulations! You have just calculated the debt-free figure that you would need if you were to take all of your time out of your work bucket and put it into your leisure bucket today. This figure is the amount of property that you would need to provide you with income and wealth for the rest of your life.

You may be looking at this figure and wondering how you could ever attempt to own so much property. Remember, this is the figure if you were to hang up your work boots today. For many, this is not realistic and for most, this exercise is not about what you want today, but what you're working toward for the future.

So let's look at the next step of the calculation – when you want it.

Step 2: Adjust for inflation – when do you want it?

If you're not familiar with inflation, it is the amount that prices rise each year compared to the last. If you think back to when you were a kid, try to remember the price of an ice cream then compare it to the price you pay today – that's inflation.

Although Australia has had times when inflation has been in double digits, historical data shows that, on average, inflation in Australia usually sits between 3% and 4%.

So why is this important? When you're looking at building a property portfolio that may not mature for another 20 or 30 years, you want to be sure that your money will bring the same value as it does in today's dollars. After all, you did calculate the amount your lifestyle would cost based on what you can buy today.

The following table provides a quick way to do this. Based on the time frame in which you want to achieve your goal, simply multiply your final dollar amount in the table above by the multiplier you see below. This is an approximate calculation that allows for inflation at the national average of 3.5%.

For example, if you wanted to hit your target in 30 years, you would multiply your property portfolio value above by three. If you wanted to hit it in 20 years, multiply it by two and so on.

FUTURE INFLATION

30 yrs = × 3
20 yrs = × 2
10 yrs = × 1.5

MY FUTURE TARGET ADJUSTED FOR INFLATION

$_____ × _____ = $_____

This is the value of the portfolio that you need to start working towards today if you are to achieve your goals for the future.

Step 3: Allow for growth – the power of compounding

You might be looking at the figure above thinking that this amount of debt-free property is still too far out of your reach. What you're not taking into account is the growth rate that this property can have over the years. What may seem like a small amount now could easily grow to hit the target that you need to reach.

In this step you adjust this figure for the growth that you can expect in the time that you are going to take to acquire your property portfolio (the same time you have allowed for inflation).

As the compounding growth calculation can get quite complicated, let's keep it simple and assume that your property portfolio will double every 10 years. This allows for a growth rate of just over 7%, which is very close to the historical average of Australian properties dating back to 1955. Remember, you're working backwards so you will halve each figure to get to the present-day value.

Whatever that target is, enter the final figure from the above table next to the year you wish to have reached your goal, then simply work down the list until you arrive at a figure for today.

The example shown is for a 30-year period, however, you can choose a different time frame. Again, keep in mind that these are approximate amounts. Don't get stuck on the detail. Just get it done and work from there.

FUTURE VALUES ADJUSTED FOR GROWTH

Property value	Example property value
30 yrs = $_____ ÷ 2	30 yrs = **$11,700,000** ÷ 2
20 yrs = $_____ ÷ 2	20 yrs = **$5,850,000** ÷ 2
10 yrs = $_____ ÷ 2	10 yrs = **$2,925,000** ÷ 2
Today = $_____	Today = **$1,462,500**

Congratulations! You have just worked out the value of the portfolio you need to acquire today to hit your target in the years to come. To be clearer, this is the value of your property portfolio that you will be looking to own debt-free to generate the level of income to remove your time from your work bucket in years to come. Write this figure below so you can see it clearly.

MY PORTFOLIO TARGET TODAY

$_____

Some of you may be looking at this figure thinking you've been a little too ambitious, while others may be breathing a sigh of relief now growth has been taken into account. The important thing is that you now have a base to work from and you can adjust these figures according to whether you feel you could achieve something better or whether your goals are out of reach and need readjusting.

Some assumptions to allow for

It's also important to remember that there are a number of assumptions with this model.

Exact figures and calculations have been done away with for the sake of producing a result that's tangible and quick to calculate. It's important not to get stuck in the detail and complexity and then never have a goal to aim for. Being 90% right, you will be able to fine-tune things along the way – it's more important to get started.

The income levels above assume you may never put time into your work bucket again. While this is a dream for many, the reality is that it can be quite boring and many people find a great affinity with their work. This strategy doesn't have to disregard your work income completely. If you feel comfortable putting 30% or 40% more time into your work bucket and relying on that income then, by all means, reduce this amount from the income targets above and work toward that.

While it may not be possible for you to attain that amount of debt-free property today, even if you were to acquire this amount of property and never pay it off, you would still be holding a substantial portfolio. In the example shown above, $11.7 million less the initial value of $1.4 million would still provide a healthy result of $10 million in property once the debt was paid down. This may be shy of your original expectations, but you would be far in front of most and you can always tweak things as you go.

Now that you have established a firm dollar figure to aim for, the next part of the book will introduce you to the strategies and tactics you will need to implement to acquire this amount of property and live your ideal lifestyle.

PART 2

CREATING YOUR STRATEGY

THINK AND GROW RICH

The investor's chief problem – and even his worst enemy – is likely to be himself.

Ben Graham

While many of you might be looking at the property goals that you have created and are keen to understand the best way of acquiring these assets, it's important to have the right mindset before you do anything.

Ask any successful investor and they will tell you that success starts with the right mindset. You may have all the knowledge in the world but, unless you have the right attitude and follow a set of sound principles, it will all be for nothing.

Principles for success

Below are nine principles that are the culmination of years of experience, both good and bad. It is a framework that can be applied to your mental attitude and decision-making processes so that you have the greatest possible chance of success.

Principle 1: Make a plan and follow it

Many people do what is called 'investing by default' – they get into an investment mainly because friends or family have told them it's a good thing to do. They give little regard to where it will get them and whether they'll be satisfied with the result when they get there.

Having a plan helps to focus on what you really want and helps you to work out the steps to get there. It gives the big picture and the reason why you're doing what you're doing while providing smaller targets to aim for along the way.

Don't be a default investor. Dream big, make a plan now and understand the steps you need to take to get you there.

Principle 2: Think long term

Ignore short-term events, think big picture, focus on a goal – these are all ideas that will help you to play a long-term game and not get caught up in the wild fluctuations that can happen so easily in day-to-day activities.

It's about making money,
not saving money.

Thinking long term gives you more clarity and insight to make strategic investment decisions, helping you to see past the emotions of the day and even to buy when everyone else can see only doom and gloom.

When it's time to throw your hat in the ring, long-term thinking allows you to sacrifice small concessions to achieve better overall outcomes. For example, you can avoid getting caught up in trying to win a negotiation for a few thousand dollars, potentially missing out on a deal that produces outstanding results for years to come. Remember, it's about making money, not saving money.

Principle 3: Follow facts, not emotions

If you hear comments or read a news piece that excites or scares you, check your emotions and do some research first. One developer going broke does not indicate a weakening market or economy. Likewise, a friend telling you that they made a fortune in mining towns or serviced apartments or luxury units does not mean that everyone can make a killing doing the same.

Find out from reliable sources whether something is true and don't fall into the trap of thinking that you have spotted a trend without substantiating the claims.

See 'Dealing with the media – help or hindrance?' on p. 31–32.

Principle 4: Take calculated risks

As an investor, you will have to accept some level of risk. If you try to avoid all risk and make sure every conceivable outcome will work in your favour, you'll end up with an investment that makes very little profit at all.

On the other hand, diving headlong into a deal without considering the potential outcomes will probably not end well. As they say, only fools rush in.

Weigh up the benefits of the deal against the potential disadvantages or losses. If the chances are high that you will come out on top and you feel comfortable moving forward, then accept those risks and take action.

There's nothing wrong in trusting your instincts or being assertive as long as you've taken a true measure of the risks involved.

One way to minimise risk is to engage an advisor or professional in the property market who is working for you to build your property portfolio.

Principle 5: Put fundamentals before price

A property investment could be held for 20 or even 30 years at a time, so making a purchase based on the fact that you can get it for a 'good price' now can leave you holding a lemon in years to come.

Always ask yourself, 'Would I be happy to own this in 30 years time?'. If you can answer 'yes' then you can start negotiating on price.

Remember, property is a long-term game so it's important to think many years forward from today. Too many people get drawn into an investment because a skilled salesperson dangled a 'bargain' in front of them.

Your first priority is to ensure your investment is ticking all the right boxes (or as many as possible) before anything else. If the property meets your chosen criteria, then you can talk about price, not beforehand. See pages 52 –59 for more about criteria for purchasing an investment property.

Principle 6: Be front foot, not back foot

When you start to work out your investment plan, get excited. Feel confident. Focus on how you're going to make it happen. When you're looking at property, be assertive, look for opportunities and have fun.

Don't hang back hoping it will happen by itself; it won't. Reluctance serves no one. If it's not a good deal, move on and look forward for the next one. If it is a good deal, grab it with both hands before some other smart investor sets their sights on it.

Being too detail-oriented can be a form of reluctance as well – getting caught up in the research and measuring one strategy against another. And what happens? You fail to take any action at all.

When you're looking at your next investment, tell yourself that this is not the last investment you will ever make. Remember, you're following a plan (see Principle 1). You're not going to make a rash decision, but you also don't have to wait until you're 110% right either.

Take the initiative. As time goes on and you look back, you'll realise it was the step that you took, rather than waiting for everything to be perfect, that made all the difference.

Principle 7: Keep it simple

You have to start somewhere. Take stock of where you are first, be mindful of the basics, keep it simple and move forward confidently in the direction of your goals.

The problem with many would-be investors is that they want to start at the top. They learn the tricks and techniques of professionals who have developed a niche system using wraps, leasebacks, options or property developments.

The trick is to start small and keep it simple. Talk to any successful investor and you will find they had humble beginnings. Even someone who appeared to be an overnight success had years of taking small steps leading them to where they are today.

Principle 8: Stay calm

Emotions will always go up and down and are usually tied to a perceived outcome that you have in mind. The investor who is slave to the whims of the emotional rollercoaster will end up making rash decisions that they will more than likely come to regret later.

If you feel yourself getting angry or excited about the outcome of an investment decision, be aware of your emotions and step back from the situation. You will be able to create a much better outcome or alternative option when you can think with a clear and rational mind.

Principle 9: Expect change

The price of property will rise and fall. No asset is immune to fluctuations. However, if you're playing for the long term, you will need to accept minor setbacks along the way as just that – minor.

Understand this and you will be better prepared for the good times as well as the bad.

In summary, understanding that success starts with the right mindset is the key to any great endeavour.

Following the nine principles outlined will put you in good stead to build your property wealth and to keep you focused. Once you're aligned mentally, the next step is to develop your skills. The next chapter will look at the different strategies for building your property portfolio and choosing the one that is right for you.

DEALING WITH THE MEDIA – HELP OR HINDRANCE?

The media can be both helpful for finding investment properties or a hindrance depending on the type of media you're viewing. It's easy to accept most reports in print or on television at face value when, in fact, the information may be quite biased.

For most media, headlines are there to sell – they need to trigger an emotional response that will make the audience take notice and want to enquire further. They do this by creating dramatic situations that often trigger emotions such as fear, greed, uncertainty or elation.

In order to do this successfully, they also need to vary the emotion. It wouldn't be newsworthy if they reported the same story over and over.

The headlines may read tragedy one week and hope the next. For example, it's not uncommon to see newspaper headings that read as follows:

Australian property bubble set to burst as US goes into meltdown

The next week's headline may then read:

House prices surge on the back of mining boom

There may be valid points to substantiate the writing of both articles, but more than likely the drama of the headline may fail to eventuate.

As much as we might like to think that the news is without bias, this is often not the case. The trick is to be aware of the rollercoaster. Don't get caught up in the emotional ride and don't fall into the trap of reacting to claims that haven't been substantiated by a variety of reliable sources.

CHOOSING
A STRATEGY

*Investing should be more like watching
paint dry or watching grass grow.
If you want excitement,
take $800 and go to Las Vegas.*

Paul Samuelson

You now have the nine principles for investing in property and, previously, you worked out the value of the portfolio that you need to build so you can start moving more of your time into your leisure bucket. However, the question remains: How are you going to get there?

The answer lies in your strategy. Strategy is simply your plan on how you're going to get to where you're going. It's a blueprint, or a roadmap that can be used to keep you on track. Your strategy acts as a yardstick to help you make the choices that will get you to your destination.

Many people are left clutching at straws when it comes to an investment strategy. There is usually no real understanding as to why they bought that particular property in that particular area for that particular price.

To develop an effective strategy, there are three main points to consider:

- understanding the difference between yield and growth
- knowing how each strategy works to create wealth
- deciding on a sustainable investment strategy that works for you.

High yield or high growth?

The return on any investment is usually divided into two parts: income and asset growth. For shares, this is seen as the dividends you may receive and the price of the share itself (hopefully increasing). For property, it is the rental income and the capital growth of the property.

The relationship between rental yield and capital growth is usually an inverse or opposite one. Typically, the stronger the rental yield, the lower the capital growth, while those properties experiencing stronger capital growth will usually achieve a much lower rental yield. Investors need to make the decision as to which strategy to pursue.

Many people will prefer one to the other or a combination of the two depending on where they are in their portfolio. So which one is right for you?

The following chart outlines the general behaviour of high-yield properties vs. high-growth properties. Keep in mind that both yield and growth are important in building a portfolio. The balance of each will depend on the strategy you decide to take.

GENERAL CHARACTERISTICS OF YIELD VS. GROWTH PROPERTIES

Yield focus	Growth focus
Lower $$ values	Higher $$$$ values
Lower growth	Higher growth
Cash-flow positive	Cash-flow negative

Lower-value properties tend to attract higher yields, especially in the capital cities, because there tends to be a floor to how low rents can go. If a property has a reasonable rent but is well under $300,000, it's reasonable to expect a stronger yield. For this reason, high-yield properties tend to be found in the outer ring suburbs or in regional areas where property prices are not as high and demand is not as strong.

Although the majority of properties bought in Australia are cash-flow negative to start with, meaning the expenses are greater than the rental income, over time many of those properties will become cash-flow neutral or even cash-flow positive as rents increase and/or the debt is reduced.

Choosing a high-yield strategy

The decision to purchase a high-yielding property can come down to a number of factors, and, just because you decide to pursue this strategy today, doesn't mean you can't change your strategy further down the line.

Few years remaining to service debt

If you're moving into retirement or semi-retirement, it can be beneficial to start focusing more on high-yield properties than on high-growth properties. High-growth properties are often cash-flow negative, taking money out of your pocket rather than contributing to your income. This lack of income in retirement can affect your lifestyle much more than if you were still in the workforce, leaving you with far fewer resources to draw upon should there be a shortfall.

High-growth properties also tend to require a longer-term commitment to the market as they take approximately 10 years to move through a full growth cycle where the gains can be fully realised.

If you move into retirement before your investment has had a chance to fully realise its gains and the investment still has a negative cash flow, then you could be forced to sell the property at a time that doesn't get the best outcome. Your efforts may be better spent purchasing a lower-value, high-yield property that will provide a good rental income regardless of the growth you may or may not receive.

Earning a lower income

High yielding properties can often be better for low-income earners simply because there may be very little extra cash flow to channel to an investment. Any additional income that can be generated from the investment is not only welcomed, it's often needed to get ahead.

As low-income earners are on lower tax rates, the tax breaks from negatively-geared properties are often less of an advantage to them as they are to high-income earners.

Generally, a low-income earner will have a lower asset base to work from, so diversification with many lower-priced properties can be better than having 'all your eggs in one basket' with a higher-priced property.

Less financial stress

Cash-flow positive properties are often favoured for their ability to make money from day one. They don't put the investor under the financial strain as cash-flow negative properties do (where you have to contribute to the investment). This can make it easier to purchase additional high-yield investments, especially for those on lower incomes, as they're not losing money with each purchase.

Keep in mind that while the rental yield must be reasonably high to create a cash-flow positive situation, it's also necessary to have relatively low interest rates. In a market where high interest rates exist, additional cash flow can be hard to come by. For this reason, it is important that you can service the debt even if interest rates rise to unexpected levels.

Yield – what to expect?

Although Australia is a big place, the numbers are generally the same across the country when it comes to rental yields. Here is a guide to rental yields in the Australian property market.

GENERAL GUIDE FOR RENTAL YIELDS IN THE AUSTRALIAN MARKETPLACE		
1% 2% 3%	4% 5%	6% 7% 8%+
Low yield	Mid-range yield	High yield

Those properties attracting yields above 6% are quite strong and would be ideal for low-income earners or for investors looking for strong rental returns once they've paid down their debt. If a lower-income earner can identify a property with reasonably strong growth and yields above 6%, it's definitely worth a second look.

A yield between 4% and 6% is considered fair for most properties but will generally result in a negative cash flow situation if you have put down the usual 10% or 20% deposit. Provided there is strong growth, this mid-range yield would be suitable for higher income earners who can take advantage of tax concessions.

Properties that generate yields between 1% and 3% tend to be premium priced properties above $1 million. There tends to be a much smaller market at this level and people are prepared to pay only so much in rent, so yields are typically much lower the higher the property's value.

Choosing a high-growth strategy

As shown in the earlier table, choosing to pursue a high-growth strategy typically means that the property is taking money out of your pocket in terms of cash flow, at least for the first five to seven years. As a result, only those higher income earners who can afford to sacrifice some income along the way can usually afford to hold these higher growth properties. In return, they're typically rewarded with a better quality investment that grows a greater amount of equity over time.

Looking for better quality property

Higher-value properties in stronger growth areas usually result in less maintenance being required and a better quality tenant who pays on time. This can mean a lot less risk and a lot less worry. Conversely, low-value properties can result in higher yields, but they may equate to lower-quality builds in lower socio-economic areas.

Earning a high income

High-income earners often have much more discretionary income and can afford to take the loss on a more expensive property in exchange for potentially stronger growth and less risk. In addition, the loss is reduced through government tax concessions (negative gearing).

While someone on a lower income may find it difficult to diversify their portfolio with a more expensive property, a higher income earner can spread their risk as they can afford to buy more higher-priced properties.

Building a portfolio

If your focus is on building your portfolio and you have sufficient time left in the market for the property to mature, your primary focus should be on growth.

Growth will provide you with the equity you need to outlay for the next deposit, which in turn allows you to purchase more property. While it's nice to have a positive cash flow from your investment, it can be a long time before that additional cash amounts to a deposit large enough to fund another purchase.

Why equity often beats income

Choosing between a high-growth strategy that generates equity vs. a high-yield strategy that generates income can have a significant impact on your portfolio. Let's take a look at the following example to illustrate.

Two friends, Marty and Frank, each purchase a property. Marty purchases for yield while Frank purchases for growth. Both are on modest incomes so their tax rates are both at 30%. After 10 years, the results are as follows.

HIGH YIELD VS HIGH GROWTH

	Frank's growth strategy	Marty's yield strategy
Property purchase price	$500,000	$500,000
Avg. growth rate per year	7%	4%
Cash flow per year	$10,000 loss	$10,000 profit
AFTER 10 YEARS		
New property value	$984,000	$740,000
Equity available	**$484,000**	**$240,000**
Cash flow position	− $100,000	+ $100,000
Cash flow after tax @ 30%	**− $70,000**	**$70,000**
Total position	**$417,000**	**$310,000**

As you can see here, when it comes to generating wealth, the growth strategy is the single biggest contributor to the creation of a property portfolio over the long term. Growth not only contributes more equity to the bottom line but it can also provide the much-needed funds required for the deposit on the next purchase.

Whether you decide to pursue a growth strategy or one based on strong yields, it will depend on the amount of time you have available in the market, your level of income and the eventual result you're hoping for. While a healthy yield eases the burden of holding the investment and can provide a steady stream of income into retirement, strong capital growth will build substantially more wealth in the long term.

Understanding the fundamentals that contribute to this growth is key to building a successful portfolio so let's take a look at the major contributing factors to growth in the next chapter.

AIMING FOR GROWTH

*Someone's sitting in the shade today
because someone planted a tree a long time ago.*

Warren Buffett

If you're to build a portfolio that will achieve the targets that you have set, your greatest chance of success will come from selecting properties in high growth areas.

Understanding the principles that affect growth will allow you to walk into any area and determine whether that area will perform well over the long term or whether the fundamentals just don't add up.

Finding properties in high growth areas

People drive demand for housing so it stands to reason that the more people there are, the more demand exists in the market as a whole. Larger populations mean stronger demand overall while smaller populations can have lagging markets.

A high growth area is one that is in demand: the more people who want to come to an area, the more demand there will be for available properties. There are a number of reasons for this.

Lifestyle areas

There are many popular places in cities, in outer suburbs and regional areas. Inner city locations tend to attract young people and empty nesters. Outer suburbs can appeal to families as they need bigger homes.

Regional towns with good employment prospects offer a quieter lifestyle. In addition, popular beach suburbs and coastal areas that offer leisurely lifestyles for residents are often in demand and will no doubt see an increase in demand in the future as Australia's demographics change.

Job opportunities

One of the strongest influences on population growth in an area is the prospect of new jobs. Mining towns have provided the quintessential example, with hundreds of new employees flocking to outback regions of Australia where barely a tumbleweed was to be seen earlier.

The might of the mining industry has effectively changed the landscape of places like Port Hedland, Moranbah, Karratha and the Pilbara to name a few. Darwin, with a population of just over 120,000 people, has experienced a surge in numbers from new liquefied gas projects and defence force infrastructure.

On a smaller scale, the relocation of large companies to areas that are strategically positioned often means relocation for the workers and their families as well.

High city rents for businesses have seen many large companies move to areas such as North Ryde in the north-west of Sydney where new infrastructure and cheaper commercial premises offer much lower overheads.

Improved facilities and infrastructure

This can include anything from new cafes and restaurants opening in an area to new infrastructure being built to link highways or train routes – this essentially improves the lifestyle or services in that area.

Most of Australia's capital cities have experienced growth in the developing fringes. As industry and infrastructure grow, the improved lifestyle in an area attracts new families. These areas become burgeoning epicentres that soon act as satellite cities to the primary city centre.

The more money that flows to an area from multiple sources, the more resilient it will be in times of hardship and the more likely the assets within that area will hold their value.

Immigration

One of the most influential factors in the resilience of Australia's property market has been the level of net migration from overseas students and temporary skilled migrants, especially in the last five years.

> ## AN INTERESTING FACT
>
> The CIA World Factbook rates Australia as no. 17 in over 200 countries for net migration levels while the Australian Bureau of Statistics attributes 54% of Australia's population growth to net overseas migration.

Many immigrants tend to move to where they can identify with their own culture so observe growing communities and their cultures, what their values are and how that might apply to the properties they look for.

It's also worth watching for government initiatives that may demand skilled migrants relocate to country areas in order to have their visas approved. This can lead to regional growth in larger centres such as the 'evocities' that have been promoted in New South Wales by government and include Bathurst, Armidale and Dubbo.

Avoid areas with oversupply of housing

Looking for properties in high-growth areas is important. Next, you need to make sure that the area does not already have an oversupply of properties which can affect your ability to rent the property you buy at a good price.

Let's look at three types of supply issues that can affect your ability to rent the property for the best price and reduce the growth potential of your investment property.

Vertical supply

Towering unit blocks may appeal to some but the supply side of the equation is often forgotten by investors. One unit block might be sufficient for the demand in the area. However, problems arise when another unit block is built, and then another. Suddenly, there is a massive increase in the supply of dwellings in that area. Those dwellings that were built only a few years ago have lost their shine and ability to attract the same interest from tenants or new buyers.

It might be possible to sustain a certain level of demand within the area, but if developers can continue to build multi-storey residential unit blocks, then increasing supply can stunt any significant price growth.

Horizontal supply

As supply can increase vertically in the inner city, it can also increase horizontally in some areas – new dwellings can be built on land released for development in low-rise suburbs and on the outskirts of the town or city.

Often developments are released in stages if the area of land is quite large. It's also more lucrative to the developer to release smaller areas first as it keeps supply limited. Staged releases can be up to 200 or 300 sites at a time.

In this model below, Lot 1 of 200 homes may be sold first, then a year later, Lot 2 will be sold and so on.

STAGED RELEASE OF HOUSING ALLOTMENTS			
LOT 1	**LOT 2**	**LOT 3**	**LOT 4**
200 homes	200 homes	200 homes	200 homes

So how might this affect the price of the homes in the area?

If you were to buy a house in Lot 1, only to find out a year later that there will be 200 houses built down the road at a price not much higher than you paid, it would be difficult to drum up demand for your property.

Properties built en masse in these large estates tend to have five or so designs that seem to run throughout the neighbourhood. This lack of uniqueness and massive increase in supply stunt the price of the older properties for many years and make it very difficult to get out of the investment without reducing the price.

Undersupply

Prices can increase for a property if supply falls (not enough properties) while the population remains the same or even increases.

Areas such as Port Hedland in Western Australia or Moranbah in Queensland experienced such massive growth in mining that the supply of houses available couldn't keep up with the surge in workers coming into town. As a result, these sleepy towns suddenly experienced double-digit property growth for years as mining employees continued to fill the town.

On a broader level, at the time of writing, New South Wales is undergoing an increasing shortfall of residential homes relative to the growing population which will no doubt put upward pressure on prices.

FINDING A PROPERTY WITH STRONG DEMAND

Look for signs of strong demand	Look for signs of limited supply	Avoid signs of oversupply
Lifestyle suburbs that remain iconic year after year	Minimal space available for further development – up or out	Inner city suburbs with multiple high-rise apartment blocks, construction sites and/ or large holes ready for development
New infrastructure, transportation routes or business parks being constructed in nearby areas	Inner city suburbs with height restrictions (look for a lack of high-rise apartments)	Land releases where new housing estates are being built or are marked for the area
Multinational companies investing in new headquarters within the area	Towns or cities hemmed in by mountain ranges, oceans, or large national parks	Regional areas with an abundant supply of land for development
Immigration and movement of people to regional centres	Planning restrictions, limited labour markets or slow approval processes may limit supply but aren't dependable as they may change over time	

FOLLOW THE BIG BUSINESSES

It's always worth noting where the bigger companies such as Woolworths, Bunnings and Dan Murphy's decide to open new stores. These companies invest a lot of money when they build new infrastructure so you can be sure they've invested a lot in their research to identify where the next areas of growth are set to occur.

Timing the market – when to buy

There's a saying that 'time in' the market is more important than 'timing' the market – meaning that the long-term benefits of staying in the market and letting the compound effect work for you are far more effective than jumping in and out trying to chase hot spots or growth spurts.

This is true on a number of levels. Firstly, because the entry and exit costs of property are so high – getting in and out of the market frequently can be costly. Secondly, no one has a crystal ball to predict when growth will or won't occur.

Growth does tend to move through phases and while chasing underperforming 'hot spot' suburbs can be quite speculative, looking for an entry point into well-established suburbs can result in good value purchases.

Take a look at these growth rates for units in Melbourne's St Kilda for example.

ST KILDA – 10 YEAR AVERAGE GROWTH RATE FOR UNITS

Year	'03	'04	'05	'06	'07	'08	'09	'10	'11	'12
Growth rate	6%	1%	4%	5%	18%	7%	8%	14%	– 3%	– 4%

Source: Residex Suburb Report; St Kilda, Jan 28 2013, www.residex.com.au

The 10-year average growth rate of St Kilda has been 5.6%. You can see from the growth rates here that from 2004 to 2006 and from 2011 to 2012 the growth rate was below this average. For the other years, the growth was above the average. In fact, this is how an average is achieved – some points lie below the line, some points above the line.

The following graph is a simplified model of how average growth works.

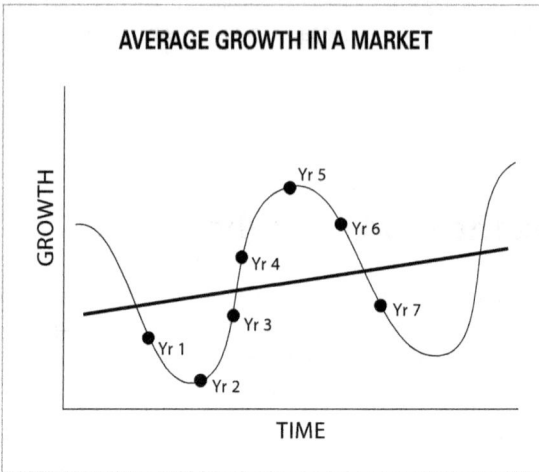

AVERAGE GROWTH IN A MARKET

GROWTH

Yr 5

Yr 6

Yr 4

Yr 7

Yr 3

Yr 1

Yr 2

TIME

Note the trend line is trending upwards, meaning that growth is increasing on average, so this suburb would appear to be doing well over the long term.

You can see there are periods of below average growth (years 1, 2, 3 and 7) and years of above average growth (years 4, 5 and 6). The variation is not about the price of properties in the area, but the growth rate that those prices have experienced.

It stands to reason that if you can identify the growth cycle of an area and purchase after a period of growth that has been below the line, you may be able to take advantage of the following years of growth to come that will occur above the line.

What growth trends mean for investors

Mapping the growth in an area gives an insight into two things: the growth trend line and when to enter the market.

Growth trend line

The growth trend line is identified by the thick line that cuts through the cycle representing the average at different points in time. As long as the trend is flat or has an upward direction, it indicates that growth is either consistent or increasing.

A trend line that is downward in direction indicates growth is slowing. In this case, prices actually plateau, or worse, begin to decline.

The direction of the trend line is essential to note as a property with a 10-year average of 8% could have a growth trend line going in any direction. It's important that each year is tracked and that the suburb has a long-term trend of steady or increasing growth.

When to enter the market

Those years below the trend line are an opportunity to buy into the area before growth really takes off. The years above the trend line might be considered overheated.

In the graph, 'Average growth in a market', year 3 would be on optimal time to enter the market. At this point, there have been a number of years of subdued growth and, while the growth rate is beginning to increase, it is still a little below the average.

Year 4 could also be a good time to buy into the area. Although year 4 experiences stronger growth, the growth rate remains relatively close to the long-term average and the preceding years show that the growth rate is increasing. Prices are clearly experiencing an increase and it is still close enough to the average not to be considered overheated.

THINK DIFFERENTLY

While this type of thinking falls back to the old adage 'buy low, sell high', it is actually the opposite of what most people do.

Most people will look for areas with the strongest growth figures and conclude that this is a booming suburb or a hot spot. They're completely right of course, but this is not the time you want to invest. Very few suburbs experience double-digit growth year on year without coming back down to earth.

Rather than just looking for the strongest growth suburbs, think about the average growth rate as well. If the average is 8% and the current growth rate is 14%, naturally it has to come back down. Conversely, when the suburb is experiencing lagging growth and no one is interested, this can be a great time to jump in and secure a deal. Not only can you get a property for a fair value, but also it positions you to take advantage of any future growth that is set to occur as it reverts to the average.

Understanding growth factors doesn't mean that yield is not important – there is no point trying to hold an asset if you can't sustain the cash flow that's needed. Maximising the amount of income that can be generated, whether you're pursuing high yields or trying to minimise your outlays, is an essential part of the investment and one which is explored in the next chapter.

MAXIMISING CASH FLOW

Cash is a fact. Profit is an opinion.

Alfred Rappaport

Whether you're pursuing a high-yield strategy to generate income or a high-growth strategy to build a strong asset base, looking for the right fundamentals that will maximise your cash flow is essential when it comes to property selection.

Simply put, maximising cash flow is all about getting the most rent (income) while keeping costs (expenses) to a minimum.

Although capital growth is essential when building a portfolio, a property that doesn't yield a decent return can quickly become a money pit that will eventually break the bank and force you to sell.

Buying a good rental property

The two most useful words that you can remember to help keep your focus on properties that attract higher rents are 'tenant appeal'.

Put simply, tenants are the people who pay the rent. They are also the people who are helping you to pay off your mortgage so buy them something nice and treat them well. If you don't, you'll always be paying an agent to find new tenants and paying additional letting fees.

It's also wise to keep in mind who your tenants are. If your market is under 30 and single, then their needs are going to be quite different from those of a family in a regional centre.

Not surprisingly, the things that you need to look for when it comes to property selection are the things that a tenant finds very appealing.

Convenience

Without a doubt, one of the biggest contributors to people renting is whether they're close to where they spend their time. This includes being close to lifestyle centres such as cafes and shopping centres as well as being within walking distance of transportation.

The number of cafes in the area is often a good sign of whether a tenant would be attracted to the suburb.

Cafes are one of the most magnetic sources of community these days – generally the more cafes that are in the area, the more popular it is.

Remember, a tenant can easily move to a better location. If you buy a house for $600,000, you're unlikely to move because there are no cafes in walking distance. It's quite the opposite for renters (especially in the cities) who are quite happy to pay an extra $20 or $30 to be closer to where they want to live.

Plenty of light

Unless you're a teen vampire (some parents do have them), most humans will gravitate toward light. Countless people have walked into a property for sale or rent that was dark and walked straight out again, muttering to themselves, 'I could never live there'.

On the other hand, a rental property with lots of light rents far more easily. A light, open-plan property will almost always be in demand and you'll likely attract a much better quality tenant.

Privacy

Although this is rarely a problem in low-density or regional areas where houses tend to dominate the landscape, it's a major consideration for those living next to or on top of each other. Higher density living doesn't suit everyone, however, most tenants appreciate privacy.

Apartments that look into the bedrooms or living rooms of the building next door or have them looking into your property are far from appealing. Best to avoid such properties if at all possible and look for those properties that allow privacy.

Outside living space

It's natural for people to want some sense of freedom in their lives and that doesn't come from feeling as though they're living in a box.

A property that has an outside area provides a huge benefit. Whether it's a back yard, a courtyard or a balcony, people prefer to have a place where they can run around, get some sun, or just greet the world in their underwear.

This is even more important if the property is located close to an outdoor lifestyle area, such as the beach. People move to these areas because they want to enjoy more of the outdoors, so don't close off your available market by choosing property that doesn't have this option.

A QUICK WORD ON FRONT YARDS, SHARED YARDS AND ROOFTOPS

As mentioned, people appreciate convenience and privacy. Front yards are rarely used these days as they lack the privacy and safety of a rear enclosed yard. In addition, shared yards or rooftops – whether they're rarely used by others or not – are not preferred by tenants. That's not to say that these spaces aren't an asset but they're never as highly prized as private space.

Scarcity

It's worth mentioning the importance of looking for some level of uniqueness about the property. Good views are excellent as there will be very few other properties that have a similar aspect to yours. The same goes for unique (but manageable) gardens or decked areas for entertaining.

Extra storage, mezzanine levels in the garage or an extra car space are also valued as some people carry a lot of gear with them and appreciate the extra room.

Other aspects of a property that make it stand out from the crowd are:

- a small, boutique block of units

- a water view

- period features

- a unique position near the beach or a park

- an oversized courtyard

- a large storage room.

Stand-out factors such as these can put a property well ahead of the market when renting and when you might want to sell.

Beware of high-rise apartment blocks where many units within the building are renting or selling at the same time. The competition can be fierce and affect rental returns and capital growth.

Avoid main roads

When it comes to convenience, think 'near', and not 'next to'. The same goes for arterial roads and thoroughfares. While people like to be able to access the main travel routes, no one likes to live on top of such busy roadways. The noise from these roads is also a turn-off even when the property is blocks away.

Improving rental income

When it comes to renting your investment, you need to focus on getting the most rent you can as well as keeping those tenants for as long as you own it (if possible).

Why do you want to keep the same tenants? Every time a tenant vacates, that property must be taken to market again. In a strong market, this is not an issue and can often lead to a rental increase. However, in a declining or soft market, this can mean the property sits empty for weeks at a time which is disastrous for cash flow. What you made in small $10 per week increments with the last tenant can be wiped out in one week.

It's also common practice for the property management company collecting the rent to take one week's rental every time a new tenant is signed on – sometimes two weeks. On a $500,000 property, that can be around $1,000 that you lose in income every time the property is leased.

Here are the most effective strategies to get the most rent from tenants and keep them happy to stay.

Increase the rent

It's not rocket science that the easiest way to get more rent is to charge the tenant more. To be more accurate, most properties on the market these days are poorly managed and are not maximising the rental income. One example is to increase the rent as soon as you buy the property (subject to proper notice) and bring the rental price back to market value. Easy money!

Always rent out in the best season

Whether your property is by the beach, in a city or town or nestled in the snow, it makes sense to rent it out when demand is at its peak. For most rental properties, the peak periods are spring and summer, except if you have a place in a snow resort. The difference in rental return can be surprising when timed properly.

If you happen to end up purchasing in an off season, try running a shorter lease or a lease for 15 months at the lower rent until you can renew the lease again at a higher amount in the peak period.

Renovate

This does require some investment and you need to be sure that you get the most bang for your buck if you do undertake a renovation.

Renovating your property will give it a new lease of life and people love moving into a place that is fresh and new. They are also more likely to stay in the property for a longer period of time as they know they may have to settle for less if they move out.

If you're going to do a renovation, it's important to make sure you're consistent throughout. Don't do a beautiful kitchen and leave the tenants with an original bathroom. Experience has shown that ad hoc renovation doesn't translate into a higher rent.

If you can't afford to renovate, a quick coat of paint, some new carpet and window dressing before advertising for a tenant can go a long way. This allows you to update the colours to keep it modern so it looks fresh and bright.

Keep it clean

There's nothing worse than trying to attract quality tenants with a dirty apartment. Most people will opt for a clean apartment any day of the week. Clean people are also the type of people you want to attract as they will look after your investment.

Allow pets (with discretion)

Let's face it, no one wants a blood-hungry Rottweiler running down the corridor of their investment property scratching up the wooden floors and scaring off the neighbours. You need to use some discretion and make sure the property manager informs you of the type of pet that the tenant might have.

These days, more and more people live alone and it's common for people to be looking for pet-friendly places. Many people will have a cat or a small dog and, with a little negotiation, they are usually more than happy to pay an additional bond to cover repairs should the animal damage anything.

Install storage

These days it's amazing how much stuff you can carry around with you. While it's not always possible to install extra cupboards, having built-ins is a must for rental properties and can be a deal breaker for people who have large amounts of clothes (about 50% of the population).

It can also be handy to create a mezzanine level in the garage if space permits. Anywhere to store those extra boxes, surfboards, fishing equipment and old tax returns is a bonus.

Present the property with professional photos

Some years ago McGrath Real Estate turned the NSW property market on its head by focusing on quality presentation and appearance. Sales went through the roof and the McGrath agents quickly found themselves hitting record sales in their areas.

It's no surprise that the best property managers are now approaching the rental market in the same professional manner. It's possible to add hundreds of dollars to the price of a rental property after a property manager takes professional photos and stages the property with furniture so the prospective tenants don't have to imagine how their furniture will fit.

Presenting your property well can massively increase the yield on your property. If your property manager tries to tell you otherwise, consider looking for another property manager.

Set realistic prices

It's a fine line between advertising your rental property at a level below market value and at a level above what it's worth.

On the one hand, your property manager may rent the property straight away, which can leave you wondering whether you could have received more money. On the other hand, the property can sit empty for weeks until you lower the price to that level that suddenly attracts the crowds.

A good property manager will be able to direct you as to what the market is expecting for a property like yours. They should also be able to provide some recent examples to back up their comments.

If you're not sure, it's always better to go a little bit under market rather than over. Being under market will usually bring a tenant straight away and you can always increase the rent at a later stage. Being over market value can leave your investment empty with no income at all.

Look at it this way. If you have a property that is worth $500 per week and you want to advertise it for $520 per week, it may sit empty for a week before you lower the rent to $510 per week. It then sits empty for another week. At this point you've lost two weeks rent, a total of $1,000, which equates to about $20 per week over the year.

In some markets, if rental demand is strong enough the prospective tenants may even bid the price up.

When it's finally rented for the market value of $500 per week, you've actually walked away with only $480 per week (allowing for the vacant weeks). It would have been much better starting at the more realistic level rather than be too ambitious.

Keeping costs low

Just as there are factors that can help maximise your income, you can also look for characteristics that will reduce your operating costs.

The following points can help you to reduce this figure as much as possible and keep costs low through the life of the investment. See also diagram, cash-flow calculator, on page 63.

Brick, not timber

Where possible, it's better to avoid a timber building. Unlike brick, which requires little maintenance and holds up structurally, timber properties require painting and can weather and decay over time. They are also subject to pests such as termites and borers that may need treatment.

Timber is usually far less energy efficient than brick and therefore timber houses are more difficult to warm and cool. This increase in utility costs can add up for the tenant.

Although many timber buildings can be attractive and hold their character, it's best to avoid them from an investment perspective.

Low strata fees

Strata fees apply for unit investment properties. They are the fees paid by individual apartment owners in a building to look after maintenance and administration of the common property of the building. These fees can sometimes be difficult to determine as the age of the buildings in some suburbs tends to make the maintenance costs for those areas much higher than others.

Strata fees are calculated on a per quarter basis – due every three months. If fees are too high, this can put a real strain on cash flow. You can end up paying thousands of dollars every few months and have nothing to show for it.

A good guide to determine whether the strata is expensive is to look at the purchase price and take three zeros off, i.e. 1%. If you have a $600,000 property, the strata fees should be about $600 per quarter, give or take 10% to 20%. This is a good guide to work with when you're doing the rounds of open for inspections.

Unless your owners' corporation is putting the funds towards something that will increase the value of the investment, such as rendering the façade or improving the overall look of the building, strata fees are a cost that will never be recovered. However, they are tax deductible as a cost of owning the investment property.

A WORD ON SPECIAL LEVIES

Special levies are those costs that are raised by the individual unit owners of a building above and beyond the normal costs of maintenance and administration. These costs can happen quite often in buildings that are old and need some major improvements.

Although the cost may seem expensive when faced with it, if the money is being used to improve the building in ways that may increase the value of the building, then paying the fee may well be worth it. Activities such as rendering the old brick façade, replacing the balcony railings with glass or even painting the building in more modern colours can increase the value and attract a better price for your property.

Also be aware that if you're buying into a building with a special levy, that levy may be the reason the other person is selling. If you can allow for that levy in your offer, then don't be afraid to make the purchase as you may end up with a great deal.

No lifts, pools, gyms or saunas

Anything that involves water is always a potential problem for leaks and anything that is mechanical and carries heavy loads will always require maintenance.

Lifts, for example, are notorious for breaking down and needing replacement. The money required to fix or replace a lift is divided between unit owners. This type of improvement does not increase the value as any potential renters or buyers expect the lift to work.

Experience shows that unit block facilities such as pools and saunas are rarely used by tenants. The extra strata fees required to maintain them rarely translate into additional rent and they end up being more trouble than they're worth.

Well kept and ordered

When buying into a unit block, you are buying into a community of sorts which can have an impact on the value of your investment.

Unit blocks that are poorly maintained or have untidy gardens say something about the majority of the owners in the building and the way they choose to run things. Reluctance to spend the necessary monies to take care of the building is often the result of short-sightedness that will cost the investor in reduced rents and poor returns when they decide to sell.

Lack of proper maintenance can also result in bigger problems which can become a significant cost. Avoid these issues by buying in a unit block that is well maintained and neatly kept – from the plants in the front garden and walkways to the well-placed signs on the noticeboards.

HOW TO BUY A GREAT INVESTMENT PROPERTY

Buy wisely	Keep costs low	Maximise rent
Close to public transport routes – trains, buses	Brick built rather than timber	Advertise for rent in the peak periods
Walking distance to cafes or corner stores	No lifts, pools, gyms or saunas	Get professional copy and photographs done when advertising
Close to shopping centres	Strata levies (for units) at approx. 1% of purchase price	Stage the property (furniture) if possible
Plenty of light (in the living rooms at the least)	Well-maintained common areas.	Renovate where possible
Balcony, courtyard or rear yard		Install storage
Privacy from others		Keep it clean
Views across the district or to the water		Allow (manageable) pets
		Maintain regular rental increases

While it's great to have a property that's growing strongly, it's critical that the investment isn't breaking the bank if you're to hold it for the long term.

Maximising the income that a property can generate is the key to this longevity. Focus on buying a low maintenance investment and always keep the tenant in mind. After all, they're the ones who will be offsetting the majority of your loan repayments. Look for convenience, look for a quality living space and always promote the property in its best light and you're bound to attract a quality tenant.

UNDERSTANDING THE NUMBERS

*Without numerical fluency, in the part of life
most of us inhibit, you are like a one-legged man
in an ass-kicking contest.*

Charlie Munger

The following calculations are essential to understanding how residential property investment works. Understanding these simple numbers will be one of the most valuable tools you will have when you ask yourself 'what will I get out of it?'.

The calculations are not designed to help you determine the value of the property or the price that you should be paying. They are designed to help you understand the costs, the income and the resulting profit as the property grows in value.

The calculations for income and expenses listed in examples in this chapter are general investment numbers only. They can vary, however, they do reflect general market conditions at the time of writing and will work for most Australian investors in the residential market today.

All figures that you're going to use are calculated as a percentage of the purchase price. This will allow you to apply these simple calculations to properties of any value.

How much does a property really cost?

There are four main elements that need to be considered in the cost of an investment property: income, loan repayments, maintenance and tax savings.

COSTS OF AN INVESTMENT PROPERTY

Income	Rent
Less – expenses	Loan repayments Maintenance
Plus	Tax savings

Let's look at each of these factors and how they impact on the cost of your investment property.

Income (rent)

This is the amount you charge your tenants for using the property. At the moment, 5% is a fair rate for a rental return. For low-value properties, this value may be closer to 6% or 7%, while for top-end properties, the value may be closer to 3% or 4%.

The value is calculated by dividing the purchase price by the total yearly rent.

Loan repayments

By far the most influential factor in the ongoing cost of property is the interest repayments attached to your loan.

Canstar and Rate City are good reference websites for the latest interest rates:

- www.canstar.com.au

- www.ratecity.com.au

The difference between 7% and 8% interest on a loan can mean hundreds of dollars to a family every week. At the time of writing, the standard variable rate was around 5.6%. However, it's always best to be more conservative and allow for a higher rate should interest rates increase.

Maintenance

Many people fail to factor this cost in and, as a result, can have unexpected difficulty with their cash flow down the line. Maintenance can include council rates, water bills and strata fees.

Although owning a house doesn't require you to pay strata fees, you do have to pay for the upkeep of the whole building, including the yard, roof, footings and other associated costs. For this reason, 1% is a good figure to use. This 1% does not factor in major or unexpected costs.

Tax savings

Tax savings are applicable only if you are making a loss on the property, otherwise known as 'cash flow negative'. In this case you would be considered 'negatively geared' and be able to deduct the loss from your taxable income.

For example, if you were to make a loss on the property of $10,000 after yearly income and expenses were taken into account, the government allows you to reduce your taxable income by the same amount. While you still make a loss, if you are in the 30% tax bracket you are effectively reducing that loss by 30% to only $7,000.

You will find most investments across Australia have a negative cash flow when they first purchase, meaning that the repayments and maintenance costs are greater than the income received. For this reason, most property investors use negative gearing in their tax strategy, at least until rent increases begin to outpace the expenses.

Now that you have your basic income and expenses outlined, it's simply a matter of putting them into your calculator.

CASH-FLOW CALCULATOR
PURCHASE PRICE OF $500,000

Rent (Income)	+ 5%	+ $25,000
less Interest rate	– 7%	– $35,000
Maintenance	– 1%	– $5,000
Subtotal	**– 3%**	**– $15,000**
+Tax savings (negative geared)	+ 1%*	+ $5,000
Total yearly cost	**– 2%**	**– $10,000**

* calculated at 30% tax rate – at 46.5% tax rate, the total yearly cost figure would be –1.5%

This is a general guideline as to what it may cost to hold a property investment. These figures are quite conservative and you may be able to improve on the rental figure or reduce the interest rate you have available to you. The key here is to get a quick snapshot of the holding costs on a year-to-year basis.

Keep in mind that the total yearly cost shown above is a loss of 2% of the total property value, not 2% of the initial investment.

For example, if you purchased a property for $500,000, you may have had only a 10% deposit of $50,000. If the total yearly cost is 2%, this would equate to approximately $10,000 or 20% of your initial investment.

Small losses, big profits

It doesn't take a genius to notice that the above example shows a yearly loss of $10,000 – that's money out of your pocket. Why would you invest in something that was supposed to make you money when it could cost you $5000 to $10,000 or more each year?

Robert Kiyosaki, author of *Rich Dad, Poor Dad*, was known for asking this very same question – why would you invest in something that took money *out* of your pocket? The answer lies in capital growth – the growth in the value of the asset over time. Let's take a look at this concept more closely.

There are two components to an investment that can create value – the value of the asset itself and the income that asset creates.

ASSET VALUE + INCOME = WEALTH

The example shown in the cash-flow calculator is a negative-gearing scenario, that is, the investor makes a loss on the income side. Let's take a look at what happens when adding the capital growth element.

BIG PICTURE PROFITS CALCULATOR

Asset growth	+ 7%	+ $35,000
less total yearly cost (from above)	– 2%	– $10,000
Total yearly profit	**+ 5%**	**+ $25,000**

In this example, even though the property may cost you 2%, or $10,000 every year, you're experiencing asset growth of $35,000. This means that you are better off by $25,000 a year on average.

It's important to remember that these profits are not realised profits. You will have increased your overall wealth but you won't necessarily have $25,000 in your bank account at the end of the year. The reality is that until you sell or release your equity through a lending facility, you will have to pay for your holding costs from your own pocket.

That's why they're called 'big picture profits' – you need to realise the big picture to understand your profit levels and not get overwhelmed with the smaller losses that you may sustain in the meantime.

Before you start thinking that you might like to retire on a pension instead, the Australian pension for retirees in 2013 was $808 per fortnight for singles and $609 per person for couples – hardly comfortable living.

How much growth do you really need?

In order to break even with an investment like this, property growth needs to be large enough so it just covers the income costs. That means in a typical investment scenario like the one shown here, growth would have to be 2%.

TYPICAL INVESTMENT SCENARIO	
Asset growth	+ 2%
less Total yearly cost (from above)	– 2%
Total yearly profit	**0%**

It's also important to realise that property doesn't grow at an even rate. Here is an example of the growth rate for houses in Bondi Beach, one of Australia's most recognised beachside suburbs.

BONDI BEACH HOUSE PRICES – 10-YEAR GROWTH RATE 2003-2012

Year	'03	'04	'05	'06	'07	'08	'09	'10	'11	'12
Growth rate	15%	10%	1%	1%	11%	22%	-4%	9%	4%	0%

Source: Residex Suburb Report; Bondi Beach Houses, 19 May 2012, www.residex.com.au

Although this suburb's growth rate experiences rises and falls, the average growth rate is 6.9%. That's why it's important to remember that property is a 10-year minimum investment. If someone had invested in 2009, their property would have experienced only an average growth rate of 2.3%, well under the long-term average. Had they sold in 2009 when the market cycle was naturally depressed, they would have missed the following years of the upswing.

If you aren't sure whether property investment can make you money, ask yourself whether you believe the growth rate will be more than 2% per year. If you think it will, then it may yield the returns you've been looking for. However, keep in mind that property is a long-term investment – short-term buying and selling may not bring you the results you're after even in a high-growth area.

One-off costs

Capital growth is all well and good but what about the one-off costs that come from a property transaction, namely stamp duty and legal fees when you're buying, and agent fees when you're selling.

Although these fees can vary from state to state – it's always best to check with your accountant for accuracy – the following provides a good indication for future transactions.

Many people overlook these figures in a property investment, yet they can add a real slug to the bottom line if you haven't accounted for them. Unfortunately, this is money that you will never see again and will need to pay every time you enter and exit a transaction.

THE COSTS OF BUYING AND SELLING Purchase Price $500,000		
Buying costs		
Stamp duty	– 4%	– $20,000
Legal and financial fees	– 1%	– $5,000
Selling costs		
Agent fees and marketing	– 3%	– $15,000
Total costs	**– 8%**	**– $40,000**

On the previous $500,000 example, if you were to buy and sell this property you would have to sell for $540,000 just to break even. For a professional renovator or property trader, this is the cost of doing business. However, many people don't realise that they lose approximately 8% of value in the family home every time they move to a different property.

It also means that if you're looking to invest, your property has to increase by 5% at least before you even begin increasing the equity in your investment.

Offset transaction costs by adding value

Stamp duty, agent fees, legal fees are all one-off costs when you buy or sell property. These costs are expensive and unavoidable. So is it possible to offset these one-off transaction costs through other means? Absolutely.

One of the benefits of property investment is the ability to add value. This is rare in the investment world. Try improving the systems of a company you just bought shares in, or increasing the value of the gold that you may be holding. Usually increases on such investments are subject to the whims of the market and you need to roll with them.

Property is different. Property can be improved in value with something as simple as a coat of paint. In fact, the world of renovation has become so much a part of the Australian mindset that people will often pay a premium for an unrenovated property simply because they believe it has the potential to make them a profit once they make some improvements.

You can profit from renovations as long as they are done correctly. Keep the goal in mind – to increase the value of the property.

Let's take a look at the following example.

AN EXAMPLE OF INCREASING VALUE IN YOUR PROPERTY		
Property value	$500,000	
Renovation	$50,000	10% (allocated budget)
New property value	$590,000	18% (increase in value)
Value added	**$40,000**	**8%**

With a $50,000 renovation, the value increased by $90,000, adding an extra $40,000 to the value of the property. By manufacturing an increase in value to this property you will have generated an additional 8% in equity that can then be used to offset your one-off transaction costs such as stamp duty and legal costs with a little left over.

Keep in mind that, even with this increase in value, if you were to sell or 'flip' the property for a profit, there would be very little in the kitty after the sales agent costs were taken into account and any gains would be subject to maximum capital gains tax (CGT). That's why it can be far more effective to hold the property and unlock the gains through an equity release once the renovation is complete. In this way you get the best of both worlds – you can access the profit, avoid capital gains and benefit from the future capital growth for years to come.

USING EQUITY
TO BUILD YOUR
PROPERTY PORTFOLIO

A journey of a thousand miles
begins with a single step.

Lao Tzu

You've worked out the value of the portfolio you need to build to achieve your goals in the long term, you know how to maximise your cash flow on a property and you understand how the numbers work when buying and selling property.

Now it's a matter of finding out how to build a portfolio using equity. The key to buying property and building your portfolio – unless you have a money tree – rests on your ability to borrow money.

This is decided by two factors:

- finding money for a deposit

- making the repayments.

While your ability to make the repayments on the loan will come largely from your own income, it is the larger task of finding the money for a deposit that will provide the biggest hurdle.

There are a number of ways to gather a deposit – borrow money from friends and family, collect an inheritance, win the lottery. In reality, there are three main ways for you to come up with this somewhat large sum of money.

FINDING MONEY FOR A DEPOSIT

Save your money	The good old-fashioned method – this is the hardest path when it comes to getting a deposit together. It is usually reserved for first-time buyers who have no other choice, or high-income earners who can't find ways to spend it fast enough.
Sell some assets	A much easier strategy – sell assets that you already own and use the profit for a deposit. This is not the most efficient strategy as selling assets can trigger capital gains tax and a number of other factors. See chapter, Understanding the numbers, pp. 60–68.
Use existing equity	If you already own property and have equity in that property then it can be as simple as asking your lender to make those funds available to you.

Using existing equity, as mentioned above, is by far the best way to finance and build your property portfolio. So let's look at how equity works and how it can be best used to your advantage.

How equity works

Equity is the amount your property is worth less the amount you owe on your mortgage. It is essentially what you would receive if you decided to sell tomorrow and pay off your loan. It is this portion that you can use to grow your property portfolio.

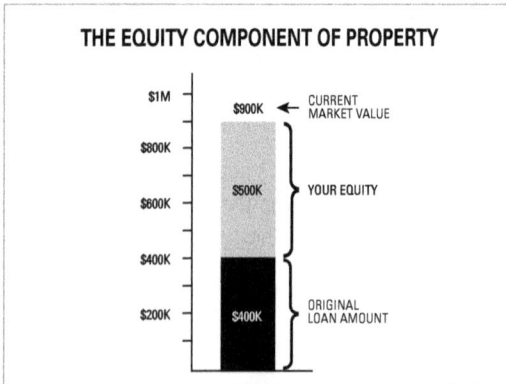

THE EQUITY COMPONENT OF PROPERTY

$1M
$900K ← CURRENT MARKET VALUE
$800K
$500K } YOUR EQUITY
$600K
$400K
$200K $400K } ORIGINAL LOAN AMOUNT

In the previous illustration, the $500,000 is the equity in this particular scenario. The attitude most people have to equity is that even though it might belong to them, it can be quite difficult to access and would actually increase their debt if they were to use it. This is true. If you choose to borrow your equity from the bank rather than sell, then you must pay for the privilege through interest repayments. But when understood and managed properly, it can also be the key to building a successful portfolio.

In his book *Rich Dad, Poor Dad*, Robert Kiyosaki wrote that a home is not an asset, as people always need a home to live in, so it can't be used to grow your wealth. The fact is that after years of paying down the mortgage, equity in the family home can be used to leverage into additional investments to build your portfolio. In turn, your portfolio grows in value as you move towards achieving your goal of financial freedom.

Accessing equity

The amount of equity that you can access usually depends on the amount that your bank is willing to lend you against the original loan. If you were originally approved for a loan of up to 80%, chances are you can usually also access 80% of your equity.

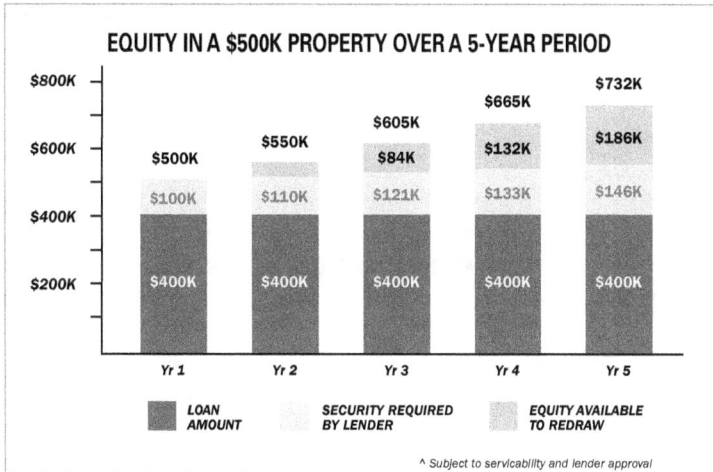

EQUITY IN A $500K PROPERTY OVER A 5-YEAR PERIOD

^ Subject to servicability and lender approval

In the previous example the loan is interest only, so the value of the $400,000 loan stays the same as the data is based on an interest-free loan.

Our lender continues to hold 20% of the value of the property as security. As the value of the property increases, the amount the lender holds as security also increases.

The equity available to withdraw is the amount that is left once the value of the loan and the amount that the lender requires as security have been taken out. Note that this is not the total equity, just the amount available to use. The total equity also includes the amount the lender is holding for security.

As you can see in this example, after 10 years there is a substantial amount of equity in the property which can be accessed. It is this equity that can be used to fund the deposit for the purchase of the next property.

Using equity to buy your next property ... and the next

Many people struggle with the idea of using equity to fund another purchase. The concept of using borrowed money to borrow more seems like the GFC all over again. While it does result in 100% of the funds being borrowed, it's important to understand that you're simply borrowing against that part of the property that you own outright. If your property has risen in value, you could sell tomorrow and those funds would be available to you once tax had been taken out.

So how much do you need in equity in order to purchase another property?

The following example looks at a $500,000 purchase and the necessary costs involved.

BUYING YOUR SECOND PROPERTY FOR $500K		
Property purchase price		**$500K**
Deposit required	(20%)	$100K
Stamp duty and legals	(5%)	$25K
Amount required for new purchase		**$125K**

To work out when you have enough equity in your property to purchase another investment, first calculate the cost of purchasing the next property (shown above). In this case, the total cost to you would be $125K.

Now it's simply a matter of working out when you have that amount of equity available to access.

Taking the same graph you saw earlier, the graph below has been adjusted to show only the available equity on the positive scale. This way you can see exactly when you have the funds that you need to purchase.

As each year passes, the equity grows and the amount available to access increases. The dotted line represents the $125K required for the next purchase.

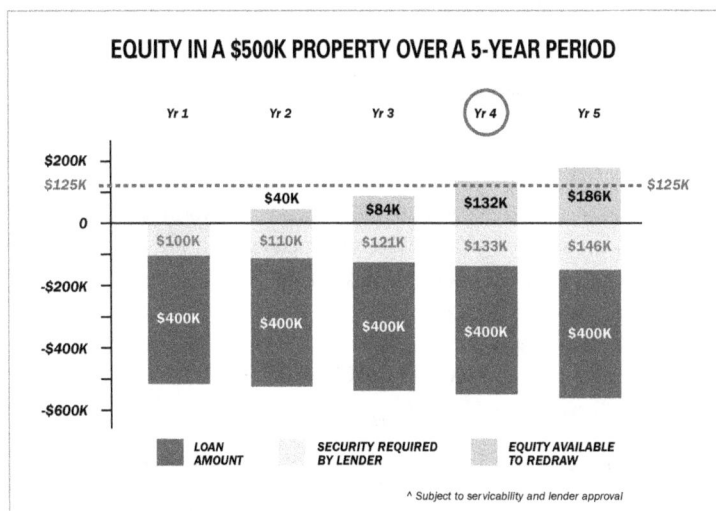

EQUITY IN A $500K PROPERTY OVER A 5-YEAR PERIOD

	Yr 1	Yr 2	Yr 3	Yr 4	Yr 5

$200K
$125K -- $125K
$40K $84K $132K $186K
0
$100K $110K $121K $133K $146K
-$200K
$400K $400K $400K $400K $400K
-$400K

-$600K

LOAN AMOUNT	SECURITY REQUIRED BY LENDER	EQUITY AVAILABLE TO REDRAW

^ Subject to servicability and lender approval

You can see that this amount is reached in year 4. This indicates that in the fourth year you will be able to purchase your next property simply by accessing the equity available in your current property.

In reality, market growth does not occur at a consistent rate so it's good to keep an eye on when the market is moving and by how much you think your property has increased in value. As soon as you feel you have enough equity to make the next investment, start talking to your lender. Alternatively, you can choose to have your properties valued each year so you know when you're due to make a move.

How much equity do you have?

Many of you may have equity in your current home that can be unlocked to use for further investment. The equity calculator below lets you work out how much equity you have available to access using the three factors: property value, loan and security.

HOW THE EQUITY CALCULATOR WORKS

+ Property value	How much is it worth today?
– Loan	How much do you still owe?
– Security	Amount required by the lender as security (e.g. 10% to 20% of property value)
= Equity available to access	

In the following example where the property is worth $500,000, the remaining loan amount is $300,000, the security with the lender is 20% ($100,000), and the equity available is $100,000.

EQUITY CALCULATOR

		My equity	Example
Property value	+	_____	+ $500,000
– Loan	–	_____	– $300,000
– Security	–	_____	– $100,000
= Equity available	=	_____	= $100,000

In the middle column, put in the figures for your equity in your current property.

Accessing equity with your lender

Once you have calculated how much equity you can withdraw, you need to be able to gain access to it.

You can do this in two ways:

- establish a line of credit (LOC) with your lender
- refinance with a new lender.

Establishing a LOC with your existing lender

This is the easiest way to access your equity as you already have a lending relationship in place and it will require far less paperwork than if you were to refinance with a new lender.

A LOC is like a bank account and you can simply transfer money into and out of the account the same way as a regular account.

Even though the equity belongs to you, the lender is allowing you to access these funds without having to sell. Your lender still needs to make sure that you can meet the repayments on this additional loan.

A LOC is a much more flexible arrangement than a standard loan. With a LOC, the money you take out of the account is considered 'borrowed money' and the bank will charge you interest only on the amount you withdraw from the account, not the amount that your lender has allowed you to access.

If you wish to deposit money back into the account, the interest charges are reduced to the amount that's still outstanding.

Refinance with a new lender

If your existing lender does not allow a LOC to access your existing equity, you can go to a different lender and apply for a new loan. If approved, the lender can take on the loan from the old lender and may increase it further to allow you to unlock the equity you have in the property.

Although this can be a worthwhile strategy if your current lender is being difficult, establishing a new loan can mean going through the whole loan application process again. This can be time consuming and you may not end up with the best deal if extra fees apply. However, you may end up with a new loan that has cheaper rates, minimal set-up fees and a host of other features that you may have missed out on previously.

Using equity as a tool

Now that you've discovered how to access your equity to cover the costs of purchasing your next property, let's look at how you can use equity in other areas.

At this point, it's wise to remember that, even though the equity belongs to you, accessing equity still requires that you borrow money. You must make sure that you can handle any extra repayments if you are to build a portfolio responsibly.

Using equity as a buffer

One of the most effective ways of reducing financial stress or making up for mortgage shortfalls is by using a LOC as a buffer. Because this is like an additional bank account, money can be accessed to pay for strata fees, council rates, mortgage shortfalls and any other expense so that you don't have to access your income or savings.

If you are going to borrow to pay back 'borrowings', you need to make sure that the asset is appreciating at a faster rate. It's all well and good to maintain your quality of life without sacrificing your income, but if your assets aren't growing and you're increasingly drawing on credit, you will go backwards very quickly.

Improving your quality of life

Using credit cards or other debt to pay for luxuries and lifestyle is like drinking seawater to quench your thirst. Holidays, a new television, a new car – these things may improve your quality of life for the moment, but borrowing to pay for them is actually making you poorer. They will eventually end, depreciate or break down and you will be left paying the debt with nothing but your own time and labour. Better to invest your time to build an active asset – your next property.

Using the equity from an appreciating asset like property can be a much better option to improve your lifestyle. While you're still paying interest to access your equity, the interest rates are a lot lower than short-term debt options like credit cards.

Using cheap debt to pay off expensive debt

If you have outstanding credit cards or a personal loan that carries a high rate of interest, it may be wise to use your LOC to pay down this debt. Your credit card debt may be costing 18.5%, however, your LOC may be costing the standard home loan rate of 7%. This difference in interest can sometimes mean the difference between getting ahead and just staying afloat.

This example shows the difference between using your credit card rather than your LOC with the same repayment amount.

PAY OFF DEBT FASTER		
	Using credit card	Using a LOC
Amount of debt	$2000	$2000
Interest rate	18.5%	7%
Monthly repayment	$41	$41
Repayment lifetime	7 yrs 5 mths	4 yrs 10 mths

Using the LOC, paying the same amount monthly, you pay off the debt 35% faster just by changing the source of debt – quite a difference.

To see how long it can take to pay your credit card, check out the ASIC Money Smart Credit Card Calculator at www.moneysmart.gov.au.

Keep in mind, if you have had difficulty controlling debt in the past then swapping one debt for another, whether it's less expensive or not, may not solve your problems.

It's also important to realise that there is an opportunity cost in using your equity to pay for debt. Your money may be better invested in growing assets rather than trying to minimise a troublesome credit card repayment.

Using your equity to add value

One of the benefits of property investment is the ability to add value. This can be rare in the investment world. Try improving the systems of a company you just bought shares in, or increasing the value of the gold that you may be holding. Usually increases are subject to the whims of the market and you need to roll with them.

Property is different. Property can be improved in value with something as simple as a coat of paint. In fact, the world of renovation has become so much a part of the Australian mindset that people will often pay a premium for an unrenovated property simply because they believe it has the potential to make them a higher profit.

Increasing profit from renovations is possible if the renovations are done correctly. As an investor, you want to increase the value of the property through a simple renovation.

Let's take a look at the following example.

VALUE ADDING FROM RENOVATION		
Property value	$500,000	
Renovation	$50,000	10% (allocated budget)
New property value	$590,000	18% (increase in value)
Value added	**$40,000**	**8%** (total value added)

With a $50,000 renovation, you have increased the value by $90,000, adding a net value of $40,000 to the value of the property (value added 8% in equity). This can offset 'one-off' transaction costs such as stamp duty and legal costs or it can be used as a deposit for the next property. Renovations can super charge your investment strategy as you don't have to wait for the natural growth of the area to take hold.

Keep in mind that, even with this increase in value, if you were to sell or 'flip' the property for a profit, there would be very little in the kitty after the sales agent costs and Capital Gains Tax (CGT) are taken into account. That's why it can be far more effective to hold the property and unlock the gains through an equity release further down the track.

PLANNING
EXIT STRATEGIES

Our favourite holding period is forever.

Warren Buffett

Before looking at the big picture scenario of how you might sell down part or all of your portfolio to achieve your end goals, it's important that you look at the process and costs of selling property.

When it comes to selling in general, there's an investment philosophy that many long-term investors tend to follow – never sell.

Warren Buffett, one of the greatest legends in the financial markets, reasons that selling incurs costs that reduce the overall value of assets. That may be true when investing in shares but it's even more so in the property market where it is far more difficult to change direction if you see a better opportunity.

The consequences of selling

While there will always be exceptional circumstances for selling, for the most part you can do far better by choosing the right property to begin with and sticking with it. If you were to sell, here are some of the major considerations that you need to take into account.

Selling incurs transaction costs

As you saw on page 66, the one-off transaction costs that come from selling property can be steep, more so if you're looking to buy back in to the market at a similar price once you've sold.

Let's recap quickly on those costs.

THE COSTS OF BUYING AND SELLING

Selling costs (agent fees):	3%
Buying costs (stamp duty and legals):	5%
Total costs:	**8%**

Many people overlook these figures in a property investment yet they can add a real slug to the bottom line if you haven't accounted for them as the following shows.

THE COSTS OF BUYING AND SELLING
Purchase Price $500,000

Buying costs		
Stamp duty	– 4%	– $20,000
Legal and financial fees	– 1%	– $5,000
Selling costs		
Agent fees and marketing	– 3%	– $15,000
Total costs	**– 8%**	**– $40,000**

If you buy and sell three investment properties within a 10-year period, you effectively reduce the value of your holdings by 24% (3 x 8%) compared to someone who simply held on to their original property.

This point alone supports why you need to choose a quality property from the start. The cost of turning over property in your portfolio may be more than you anticipated.

Selling incurs tax

If you're buying property as an investor, any profit you make on the property when you sell (less costs) is called a 'capital gain' and is subject to CGT.

CGT is not a tax rate in itself. Rather, it takes the profits from the sale of the property and adds them to your taxable income. This can often move your income levels into one of the highest tax brackets available, leaving you to pay out nearly half of all your profits in tax.

Depending on the nature of the property and how long you have owned it, you may be eligible for an exemption from this tax. The information below shows the percentage that may be applicable for CGT.

CAPITAL GAINS TAX

Owned investment property for ...	CGT
less than 12 months	**100%** of profits added to taxable income
more than 12 months	**50%** of profits added to taxable income

Note that this is for investment property only. Any capital gain you make on your home is 100% exempt from CGT so you pay no tax on the capital gain.

IS IT A HOME OR AN INVESTMENT?

It can be a contentious issue as to whether a property is considered a home or an investment, especially when the tax owing can amount to hundreds of thousands of dollars, as a principal place of residence (PPOR) is free of any capital gains tax when sold.

As a general rule, the ATO says that if you have lived in the property for a minimum of six months from the date of purchase then the property is considered to be your PPOR for the next six years whether you decide to rent it immediately after that or not.

This is only applicable for one property though. You are not allowed to claim a second PPOR which means you must be renting elsewhere. If this were the case, there would be no CGT payable if you were to sell.

If, on the other hand, you purchase the property and have a tenant move in immediately for any period of time, the property would still be considered an investment and you would be liable to pay CGT. This would be the case even if you were to move in afterward and live there for the remainder of your ownership.

So while it's wise to ensure you're paying the legitimate rate of tax to the ATO, there are definite advantages to moving into a property and claiming it as your PPOR, even for a short time, before renting it out.

Selling reduces the compounding effect

Not only does selling increase your transaction costs, which ultimately decreases your net worth, but it also can mean that you will be out of the market for an extended period of time unless you buy again shortly.

If the market is flat, normally, this would not be a problem. However, if the market is moving upward then you are missing out on the compounding price growth that your property would have been experiencing had you still owned it.

Remember the investment philosophy that many long-term investors tend to follow – never sell.

When selling could be your best option

As much as there is an argument for never selling, there may always be a case for selling and moving on. Assuming you're not looking to head for the hills and you still want some involvement in the market, here are some of the most valid reasons for cutting loose and accepting the costs.

It's a dog

Not a real dog, but a lemon. A dud. A property that has given you more headache and trouble than it's worth. This may be due to poor building works where the property has leaked, cracked, fallen over or generally left you with massive liabilities that you would rather not think about.

Or maybe it's just been poorly managed and you haven't had the ability to deal with your 'tenants from hell'. If this is the case, best to free your mind, take whatever value still exists by selling and move on.

Clean swap for a better opportunity

This is a contentious point, as what you think is an underperformer, may in fact just be a lull or a deflated period of growth. As mentioned earlier, it can be very difficult to determine when the next growth phase will be and the transaction costs alone can be a major deterrent. However, if you think that there is no hope for the property and the grass is greener in another area, sell and move on.

Reduce debt levels

One of the biggest reasons for most people selling up is to reduce debt to a level that they're comfortable with. There's certainly nothing wrong with this – your circumstances can change throughout life and the risks you took at one period of your life may be very different from what's happening today.

Sometimes releasing the debt burden by stepping away from the market, substantial growth or not, can be the best thing for your peace of mind. Don't feel bad. Recognise the situation for what it is, make the call and understand that you can always come back into the market when you're ready.

Always keep in mind that debt is a tool. You can use it to build something great or you can shoot yourself in the foot and cause some real damage. It all depends on how you manage it.

Nearing the end – hold or sell?

After many years of investing, hopefully you now have a property portfolio that has achieved your goal or even outperformed your expectations.

If you have invested for strong capital growth, you would have grown your asset base considerably and over time those properties would have become cash-flow positive as the rents started to outpace the mortgage repayments.

If you have invested in a high yield, positive cash flow property from the outset, then you may not have seen the same growth in your asset base. However, your rental yields would have been positive for many years providing you with a healthy income.

The following scenario reflects these two different outcomes – one focused on capital growth, where three properties were purchased over a 10-year period with low yield; the other focused on high yield, where five cheaper properties were purchased over the same period but achieved a lower rate of growth.

HIGH-GROWTH VS. HIGH-YIELD - A COMPARISON OVER 25 YEARS

High-growth investor			High-yield investor		
10-year growth rate		7%	10-year growth rate		5%
Rental yield (less costs)		4%	Rental yield (less costs)		7%
Results			Results		

Purchase	Loan value	After 25 years	Purchase	Loan value	After 25 years
Today	$500K	$2.71M	Today	$300K	$1M
Yr 5	$500K	$1.94M	Yr 3	$300K	$877K
Yr 10	$500K	$1.38M	Yr 5	$300K	$796K
TOTAL	**$1.5M**	**$6M**	Yr 7	$300K	$722K
			Yr 10	$300K	$624K
			TOTAL	**$1.5M**	**$4M**

Total asset value	$6M	Total asset value	$4M
Less total debt owing	$1.5M*	Less total debt owing	$1.5M*
Net assets	**$4.5M**	**Net assets**	**$2.5M**
Rental income after 25 yrs	$240K per yr	Rental income after 25 yrs	$282K per yr
Less repayments at 7%	$105K per yr	Less repayments at 7%	$105K per yr
Less maintenance at 1%	$60K per yr	Less maintenance at 1%	$40K per yr
Net income	**$75K per yr**	**Net income**	**$135K per yr**

* assuming Interest Only loan

The investor who focused on high capital growth has ended up with a higher asset base relative to the high-yield investor, while the high-yield investor has ended up with a stronger income. Remember, these numbers don't factor in inflation so the real values would be slightly less.

Assuming that you have come to the end of your investing life and did not wish to grow your portfolio further, you could decide to:

- continue to hold your investments, live off the income and watch your assets continue to appreciate

- sell some of your assets to reduce your loan amount and live debt free.

Holding on

Using the example shown above, there is a strong case for continuing to hold your investments and watch them grow.

ADVANTAGES OF RETAINING YOUR INVESTMENT PORTFOLIO

High capital growth investor		High-yield investor	
Total asset value	$6M	Total asset value	$4M
Avg. asset growth at 7%	$420K per yr	Avg. asset growth at 7%	$200K per yr
Net income	$75K per yr	Net income	$137K per yr

As you can see, the average the appreciation of your assets year on year would actually be outpacing the amount of income being generated.

As the total value of your assets continues to grow, the level of gearing also reduces, effectively reducing your risk levels to your lender. This can be beneficial if you were looking to borrow further or draw down on equity levels to create a buffer.

Selling down

Assuming you have Interest Only loans and retained your original debt levels, you may want to reduce your exposure to debt and lower your risk. While your net income is well in excess of your repayments, that could change if interest rates rise to unsustainable levels, swallowing up the majority of your rental income.

If you wanted to reduce your debt, all you would need to do is sell down some of your current holdings – enough to allow for the repayment of your original loans as well as any CGT that you may have to pay.

To calculate this you would simply add the value of all your loan amounts outstanding on each property, then decide which property or properties to sell in order to reduce this debt to a comfortable level. Once the funds from the sale of the property came through, you could simply pay down the debt on the others and enjoy the income they generated debt free.

So while there are legitimate reasons for selling property, much of the time it can be far more beneficial to retain the asset and take advantage of the long-term growth prospects. By doing this, you not only avoid the high entry and exit costs that come with buying and selling property but you also stand to gain far more in capital appreciation each year that you have invested.

Whatever your intention, make sure you're aware of all the considerations that come with property ownership and that you've consulted your accountant or planner to determine a strategy that's right for you.

PART 3
MAKING IT
HAPPEN

THERE'S NO 'I' IN TEAM

If you think it's expensive to hire a professional to do the job, wait until you hire an amateur.

Red Adair

When it comes to investing successfully, there is no point going it alone, and, if you're time poor, you're doing yourself a greater disservice than you know. Your time is far more valuable than having to learn the tricks and trade of the five or six other professionals who specialise in putting property deals together.

The following professionals are the most valuable advisers you can have in your property team. These are the people who will provide guidance and who will have the most significant positive effect on the outcome of your investments.

There are other people involved – builders, valuers, solicitors – but their involvement is usually limited to the deal itself rather than advising on strategies to increase your wealth.

Find an accountant

Whether you're an employee, business owner or investor, accountants are worth their weight in gold to you. They will be the managers of your money and will put a structure to your financial matters whether you realise you need it or not.

However, not all accountants are created equal. There are accountants who specialise in particular types of industries, such as the medical or music industry, and those who have a talent for particular types of investments, such as property. Any accountant can do a tax return, but those who know property will know how it should be purchased, work out what is affordable for your circumstances, know what deductions you can take advantage of and even what type of property will be best for your portfolio based on your personal circumstances.

Do not underestimate the power of a top-notch accountant. If you're serious about buying property for years to come, paying for quality advice now could save you tens of thousands of dollars later.

HOW TO SPOT A GOOD ACCOUNTANT

They're familiar with the industry you work in and aware of best practices to help you save money and protect against financial loss.

They suggest ways to save on tax and structure your financial assets.

They're proactive – they call you rather than you having to call them.

They're part of a professional body such as the Institute of Chartered Accountants Australia (ICAA) or Certified Public Accountants (CPA).

You can communicate with them and you're on friendly terms – remember, the wealthier you get, the more time you will be spending with them.

Look for 'award winners' in newspapers and magazines while you're waiting in lobbies.

... AND WHAT NOT TO DO

As a general rule, it's best to avoid getting involved in the following scenarios:

hiring a friend or family member – this also goes for 'mates' who have just graduated or are well-meaning people in your life trying to do you a favour

choosing an accountant because their office is close to your work or home – geographical placement has no bearing on their ability to manage your finances

choosing an accountant because they have a fancy office – you will more than likely be paying for that fancy office

choosing an accountant because they don't have a fancy office – signs of austerity do not represent competence so treat all equally and choose on their ability

Find a mortgage broker

According to Mortgage Australia Group, between 30% and 40% of people use a mortgage broker when obtaining a home loan – and the percentage is growing. You may ask, 'why use a mortgage broker who sources finance from the banks as well as other lenders so wouldn't it be better to go direct to the banks?'. To understand where the advantage lies, it's best to understand how the system works.

Firstly, a bank sells a product (money) like any other company and they are keen to sell to you as long as you can both come to an agreement on the sale of that product.

Like any business, if you were to buy in bulk or on-sell the product to other consumers, you may be offered a wholesale rate. This is essentially how a mortgage broker operates. They buy the same products from the banks that you can, but they get it a lot cheaper. They then sell it to their customers for the same price the banks do.

But if they sell it for the same price, doesn't that mean they're competing against the banks? Well yes, but the bank still wins as they now have another business out in the market selling their product to customers they may not have had access to.

Why use a broker?

Here are some of the differences between a bank and a broker.

Greater product choice with a broker

As a general guide, a bank will have about 10 or 11 products that they may be able to offer you as a lender. A broker will have access to about 200. You won't need that many of course, but it stands to reason that you will have a far better chance of getting a loan that best suits you if you have greater choice.

Even though a mortgage broker may have access to many lenders, more than likely they will only use seven or eight. That's because they can usually find what they're looking for from a handful of lenders and, not surprisingly, the more they work with those lenders, the more those lenders are likely to offer them better deals which they can pass on to you.

LOYALTY IS YESTERDAY'S NEWS

It's a mistake to think that just because you've been with a lender for years, they're going to give you the best deal. It's a competitive industry and not all lenders are created equal. Customer loyalty is a thing of the past when you are looking for the best deal so don't feel you need to return any favours. If they offer you a deal, great, if not, move on.

On the other hand, brokers can be quite ambitious with their lending and may be successful in securing you a loan for an amount far beyond what you thought you could get. Make sure you understand what your financial responsibilities will be and whether you're comfortable making repayments at that level. Only you will know whether that increased level of debt is something you will be comfortable with.

Finally, your bank may not be willing to give you the funds you're looking for. This doesn't mean that other lenders won't. Keep your options open and go with the best deal for you.

Save time with a broker

Who has the time to go to each bank and ask what types of loans they're offering? It's far more efficient to use a broker who knows the majority of products on the market and which one is best for you. It's like having your own personal shopper. And if you're worried about the cost, don't be. There is no charge for using a broker.

Access lenders who will approve your loan

Lenders use different criteria when it comes to how much they will lend to you. Some lenders will take the full amount of rental income into account; others will take 80%. Some lenders are happy to work with people who are self-employed, others aren't. This can mean the difference between being declined by a lender and happily being offered hundreds of thousands of dollars. Brokers are professionals who understand these differences and will put you in front of the right people first.

To conclude, a mortgage broker is like your personal shopper in the
mortgage market. They'll do all the legwork, they don't cost anything to use
and they'll do the job far better than you ever will.

Find a buyers agent

There's a saying that you make your money when you buy, not when you sell.

Buying well is fundamental to increasing your wealth as you build your
investments in property. Yet, for all the steps involved in successful property
investment, most investors will choose not to engage a professional at this
level and take the DIY approach instead.

Admittedly, the role of a buyers agent or buyers advocate is new to the
Australian market so it is little wonder people find the term foreign, much
less be prepared to engage them.

To shed some light on the profession, a buyers agent acts in the same
capacity as a stockbroker does for the sharemarket. If looking to buy shares,

for example, people call a stockbroker for advice about the stockmarket, advice on the best strategy, help with executing the deal and even managing their portfolio.

A buyers agent will do the same thing in the property market. They locate suitable properties that are available through both public and private sources and they negotiate the best property deals on your behalf. A buyers agent will represent you when dealing with professional selling agents who are doing their best to get top dollar for their vendors.

Buyers agents get paid in much the same way as a sales agent – typically 2% of the property transaction. However, many are paid a flat fee so the client can be assured that there is no vested interest in paying a higher price.

What a buyers agent can do for you

Like any profession, using a buyers agent provides you with a number of advantages.

Access to off-market purchases

While you may have limited time to peruse the property market, buyers agents spend most of their time inspecting properties and talking to selling agents. This gives them the privilege of being able to establish good relationships and gives them the inside edge when it comes to finding properties before they hit the market. They can secure quality properties before the general public has even had a chance to see them.

You may wonder why anyone would sell a property before taking it to market. This can happen for a number of reasons.

- The seller may not want people coming through their home for the next four to six weeks and may find it quite nerve-wracking and inconvenient.

- The seller may not want to outlay advertising and other costs associated with selling a property through a real estate agency.

- The seller may want to keep the sale of their property private.

- The property may not be fit to advertise due to its condition.

- The seller may be in a tight financial position or may be going through a divorce and needs to sell quickly.

For those buyers who do have a track record of buying quickly and for a fair price, the situations above can provide an opportunity to be shown a property without necessarily having to go through the full sales campaign to buy it. In this case, a buyers agent with good relationships with selling agents is the perfect solution.

Saves you time

While time and the need to invest in assets early is the essence of this book, it's no surprise that engaging or outsourcing to a professional for one of the most time-consuming and critical tasks of purchasing is a no-brainer. Who has the time to scour the market and educate themselves on market prices only to then have to tackle the market every weekend, travelling from one property to another only to find that the property looks nothing like the photos in the sales material?

Get your weekends back and hire a professional to show you how you can get the best result for what will probably be one of the biggest investments in your life.

Provide expertise

The market is littered with investors who invested in the wrong place at the wrong time for the wrong reasons.

Buyers agents who specialise in investments are familiar with growth areas, which properties rent well and which don't, market trends and fluctuating growth rates. They recognise value even after the sales agent's 'spin' has wained.

While some investors may look at the cost of using a buyers agent as unnecessary, others will realise that the experience and expertise of a buyers agent will provide them with a property that will typically outperform the market and will make them far more money than they thought they could save by not using one.

Find a rental property manager

The benefits of having a competent rental manager who can source the best quality tenants and keep the rent at or above market rates will be felt for years to come. Those who are left with a less than satisfactory manager will find their investment constantly underperforming which can often result in the premature sale of a perfectly good property.

Market knowledge

As your property manager is going to be setting the market rent on your investment, it is essential that they know what they can achieve for your property once it goes to market. Ask them to provide three comparable rentals in the area so that you can gauge whether they're familiar with properties similar to yours.

Presentation and communication

If you want to get top dollar for your investment, it's best to look for a positive, vibrant and knowledgeable manager. The best managers can negotiate and communicate well and know how to promote the best aspects of your property. Are they enthusiastic when they talk about the property? Are they helpful in providing all the relevant information to prospective tenants?

Also, make sure your property manager is clean and presentable whenever you meet them. If they don't value the way they look, there's little hope for your investment once it's in their hands.

On time all the time

Pay attention to the way a property manager operates. If you've asked to meet them, did they turn up on time? If you couldn't get hold of them, did they call you in a reasonable time period or did you have to chase them? Remember, if they have trouble staying on top of their own tasks, they will probably struggle to stay on top of yours (like putting rental increases in place).

Getting what you paid for

Make sure that your property is being managed by the person you meet and not by another member of the team who may not have the experience that you would like. There's nothing wrong with having other team members involved, just make sure you know who they are and feel confident they can do the job as well. It can be helpful to ask them how much experience they have in their current role and whether they have any testimonials from past clients.

You also need to feel confident enough to call them if you have any questions or if something goes wrong. They will be your go-to person for one of your biggest financial investments so you need to know you can talk freely with them about the level of rent and the work that's needed to maintain the property.

Ongoing management

Make sure your property manager gives you clear details about how they're going to manage your property and when they will be considering rental increases. Too many property investors are disappointed with their return when, in actual fact, it was the property manager who had failed to put the rent up as market conditions changed.

Equally, make sure your manager conducts regular inspections – every three months is a good period once a tenant first signs on, then every six months after that. You don't want to find your tenants have turned the place into a zoo while you weren't looking.

Remember, a good property manager is worth their weight in gold. They will be the person overseeing one of your most valuable assets and ensuring you have a trouble-free experience owning your property, so make sure they're someone you want on your team.

FINANCE FIRST

Show me the money!

Tom Cruise – Jerry Maguire

Getting finance for your investment should be the first thing that you do before anything else. Think of it like a budget. Having a budget allows you to target the areas that you can afford while avoiding those that are out of your league.

Organising finance can take quite a bit of time because it usually involves quite a lot of paperwork. Sorting out your finances and having a pre-approval in place will avoid you entering the market prematurely and allow you to put deals together quickly because you know how much you can afford.

See also 'Finding money for a deposit' on pages 69–70 and 'Find a mortgage broker' on page 91.

Deposit – how much do you need?

When you look to purchase a property, you are required to provide a percentage of the value of the property as a down payment. The more deposit you can offer to the lender, the more commitment you show for the deal. The more commitment you have, the less risky it is for the lender to be involved and so the more likely they are to lend you the money.

There are two terms you need to understand when organising your deposit:

- loan to valuation ratio (LVR)
- lender's mortgage insurance (LMI).

Loan to valuation ratio

Sounds technical but this is simply the percentage that the lender is willing to lend you for the deal. For example, if the loan is $80,000 and your deposit is $20,000, this would make the valuation (or total value of the property) $100,000. So in this case the LVR is 80%.

The following chart provides an indication from the lender's point of view of their attitude to varying levels of LVRs in today's financial environment.

LEVELS OF LOAN TO VALUATION RATIO				
<70%	80%	90%	95%	>100%
ideal	acceptable	cautious	very cautious	generally unacceptable

Since the GFC, lenders are far more risk averse than they were back in the early 2000s and they usually require investors to have a larger deposit. Gone are the days where lenders provide loans at 100% or 105%.

These days the market generally considers 80% to be an acceptable level and anything above requires an additional safeguard from the lender, which introduces the next important term to be aware of.

Lender's mortgage insurance

If the lender considers the deal too risky past a certain level, the lender will require you to pay LMI. These days LMI will nearly always be required if your LVR is 80%.

Even though this insurance is paid by you, it is actually used to insure the lender against any default by you if you fail to pay the mortgage as required.

Many lenders are happy for you to increase your LVR to 90% or 95% if you take out LMI. However, the cost of LMI can be significant. It is worked out on a sliding scale that can vary from 1% to nearly 4% of the loan itself – paid up front.

EXAMPLES OF LMI COSTS AT DIFFERENT LEVELS OF BORROWING

Your deposit	LVR	$300K	$500K	$750K	$1M
15%	85%	$1,734	$3,775	$9,645	$12,860
10%	90%	$3,075	$6,665	$13,282	$17,710
5%	95%	$6,009	$13,325	$27,742	$36,990

So if you decided to borrow $300,000 at 95%, meaning you had to put down a 5% deposit, your lender would require you to pay LMI of $6,009. If you were to borrow $1,000,000 with only a 10% deposit, this would cost you $17,710.

As you can see, LMI for residential loans can be quite substantial, especially when you start to borrow at 95%. So what's the benefit of paying LMI?

Consider the difference between outlaying a 10% deposit on a $500,000 property, $50,000 versus outlaying 20% or $100,000. For the cost of $13,282 (see table above), you can effectively manage to keep $36,718 ($50,000 less $13,282) in your bank account which can then be used for another deposit. While LMI is seen as a cost by some, by others it is simply the cost of doing business in order to get ahead quicker.

REALITY CHECK BEFORE THE LITTLE ONES ARRIVE

If you're thinking of having a family and both partners are currently employed, it's best to apply for a loan prior to pregnancy or before the baby is showing. If a lender becomes aware that you're about to have a child, they may reconsider the income for the investment and question the ability of the household to repay the debt.

Choosing a loan

There are primarily two types of loans:

- principal and interest
- interest only.

Most people will choose the principal and interest option for the home that they live in while using an interest only loan for their investments. What is the difference?

Principal and interest loan

A principal and interest (P&I) loan is when you borrow money to buy something, pay the money back that you borrowed over time along with the interest and then you own it. Simple. No mess, no fuss and really good for homeowners who don't want to still owe their lender money when they retire.

Interest only loan

An Interest Only loan (IO) is when the borrower pays the interest portion of the repayment only. The principal portion does not get paid nor will it for the life of the loan – at the end of the loan the original amount borrowed still remains. This means that if you were to borrow $500,000 today, you would still owe that amount after 25 or 30 years.

So why choose an interest only loan when buying investment properties? Here are a number of reasons.

Reduced payments

The interest portion of a loan repayment may be large, but it's not as large as paying both the principal and interest every month. If you take a $500,000 loan over 30 years at 7%, the IO repayment is nearly $410 less every month. This extra money can be put to day-to-day living expenses or into a savings account to go toward your next property.

The interest component is higher at the start

You would think that if you were a third of the way through your loan period, you would be a third of the way through paying off your loan. Not so. The interest portion is actually much higher at the beginning of a P&I loan. For example, for a P&I loan of $500,000, rather than paying $166,000 (1/3) off your loan in 10 years, you've only paid $81,000.

As many Australians sell property in the first five to seven years, those using P&I loans have had to make higher repayments and have also had close to half their repayments pay the interest component which has only served to benefit the lender.

Only the interest component is tax-deductible

For property investments, it makes sense that you maximise your tax advantages as much as possible. As you can only claim tax deductions on the interest component of the loan repayment, then repayments on an interest only loan give you a tax deduction that could reduce your income tax substantially.

Growth will be far greater than the principal amount

Take two couples who bought in Sydney in 1970 at the median price of $18,700. Couple A purchased their house with a P&I loan while Couple B used an IO loan.

In the year 2000, 30 years later, their houses are still sitting at the median price point, only now they're worth $287,000.

Yes, Couple A will be $18,700 wealthier as they would have paid off their principal amount. However, Couple B are still very comfortable with $260,000, and if they've used their reduced payments to their advantage, they would have been able to enjoy a better lifestyle than Couple A and leverage their equity into their next property investment much faster.

If you're serious about getting into property investment for the long term to build a portfolio and believe that the market will continue to grow in the future, an Interest Only loan may be your best choice.

Features of a mortgage

It's important to realise that a mortgage is made up of more than just the
interest rate. Most people will focus on the interest because it's directly related
to how much they have to pay each month, but there are other features of a
loan that can be worth far more to your property purchase in the long term.

Here are some of the more important features of a loan when buying an
investment property.

Offset account

You can reduce your repayments with an offset account.

This bank account is linked to your loan amount in a way that lets you offset
the amount in the account against the amount in the home loan in order
to reduce the interest owing. For example, if you have a $500,000 loan
but have $50,000 sitting in an offset account, then your lender calculates
interest on $450,000 rather than the $500,000 owing. This allows you to cut
down your repayments substantially.

Should you need some or all of the $50,000, the account acts as a regular
bank account allowing deposits or withdrawals. This type of account allows
you to reduce repayments without sacrificing your lifestyle.

All-in-one loan account

This is a combined mortgage, savings and cheque account that can often
include a credit card as well. This acts in the same way as an offset account,
effectively allowing all of your funds to be combined and offset against your
mortgage repayments while still allowing you to retain your regular accounts.
Watch for any higher interest rate charges on the loan for a facility like this.

Redraw facility

Instead of having your additional funds separated into an offset account or all-in-one account, you can choose to put those funds directly toward your loan. A redraw facility gives you the ability to withdraw any additional funds should you require them.

It's a little more difficult to withdraw funds (which may be good if you're not too disciplined) as it tends to take longer and you may be limited to a certain number of redraws.

Additional repayments

A loan account that allows you to increase the amount you can pay regularly effectively reduces the life of the loan. Even increasing the frequency of repayments from monthly to weekly can have a significant effect on the life of the loan. P&I loans are the only loans that allow additional payments.

Professional package

For those of you looking to use a range of products from your lender, a professional package can be the way to go. Once reserved for professionals such as doctors and lawyers, pro packages now allow anyone with a reasonable size loan to pay an annual fee and receive discounts off a range of banking services such as credit cards, application fees, valuations, insurances and even the interest rate itself often by up to 0.9%.

Pro packages allow a variety of features to be applied (including the features mentioned above). They can also allow loan portability, switches to fixed rates, loan top-ups and repayment holidays should you need a respite in times of difficulty.

> ### AN INTERESTING FACT
>
> On a $500,000 loan at 7% over 30 years, the total interest portion is just shy of $700,000 for a total payment by you of almost $1.2 million. So, over the life of your loan, you actually pay back nearly 2.5 times the amount you originally borrowed.

Assisting your loan approval

You may not be able to instantly increase your income or dramatically reduce your expenses to increase repayments of a loan. Here are a couple of tips that can improve your position without compromising your current lifestyle too radically.

Control credit card limits

Lenders look at your credit cards as potential debt pools and will record the limit on your credit card, rather than the amount owed as debt. They then multiply this amount by up to four times just to be safe.

Do yourself a favour and get rid of any cards you don't need including specialty store cards. Reduce the limit on the cards you do need to a level that's necessary.

If you do have credit card debt, pay this off as quickly as possible. If you can show that you pay the limits off every month, some lenders won't take this debt into account.

You can also use your line of credit to reduce the payment and pay it off faster (see also Accessing equity with your lender, p. 82). Remember it's not just the debt that will hold you back, it's also the opportunity cost of putting money saved on interest into an investment.

Pay off personal loans

Personal loans aren't looked upon favourably by lenders and it's best if you can reduce them or do away with them altogether. The same goes for store lending which allows a payment plan and an interest-free period so you can buy goods, such as furniture and appliances, and pay for them later.

Both practices indicate an inability to pay for the most basic of household items. It is best to pay these off to show that you're dependable and financially responsible – the type of person lenders prefer to deal with.

Clear your credit history

Your credit history is kept on file and is accessed by any lender when you apply for a loan. Think of this as a financial scorecard. Among other things, it includes your personal details, loan and credit applications, any defaults and credit infringements.

It's essential that this record remains as clean as possible, so before you apply for a loan, order your report and check there are no unwanted or unjustified claims or errors. If there is something that you feel is unfair, contact the company, question its validity and ask them to remove it if possible.

Needless to say, it helps to pay all your bills on time. Also try to keep the number of loan applications to a minimum. Two or three applications are acceptable, but having more than that is questionable.

In Australia you can contact Veda Advantage
or go to www.mycreditfile.com.au
and order your own credit file.

Be honest about your financial situation

Finance is the backbone of building an investment portfolio. This makes your lender or mortgage broker a critical part of your team.

It's essential to be open and up front about all your financial details. Lenders rely on this information so make them aware of your financial details.

This goes for tax returns as well. Your tax returns are your official record that you can afford the debt that you're about to take on. If you haven't completed your tax returns in some time, it can be very difficult to determine whether you can afford to service the levels of debt that you're asking for.

RESEARCH AND SEARCH

*No wise pilot, no matter how great his talent
and experience, fails to use his checklist.*

Charlie Munger

You will be streets ahead to make the right purchase at the right time if you have a strategy in mind and are pre-approved for finance before you begin your search. Most people search for the property first, locate their ideal investment and then spend the next few frantic weeks trying to arrange finance before being beaten by another purchaser who is far more prepared.

Researching options

Being prepared allows you to target properties that are within your budget. So where do you start looking for your investment property?

Online

These days, online research is the single most effective strategy to find a property. An Internet search will pull up hundreds of properties with specific criteria at the touch of a button.

There are a number of sites you can use to search for property, however the biggest are:

- domain.com.au
- realestate.com.au.

One of the benefits of using realestate.com.au is that it allows you to view properties in a gallery format, has open for inspection and auction tabs and gives you the ability to search for blocks of units.

Using domain.com.au, however, allows you to search by location, which is very handy for selecting particular areas rather than one suburb.

Sales agents

Sales agents are there to match buyers with sellers and you can be sure that they're motivated to show you the properties that suit your criteria because they want to make a sale.

If you want to buy in a particular area, you'll soon realise that there are a few local agents who regularly sell the types of properties you want as you'll be running into them again and again at each open for inspection. Keep in touch with these agents, let them know what you're looking for and, if they're worth their weight, they'll bring a great deal your way.

Print media

People still look in the real estate classified sections of newspapers to find properties which is why real estate agencies still advertise in print. However, there will not be any properties in print that are not online these days.

Vendor direct

You may come across a situation where you know someone or have a 'friend of a friend' who has a property to sell. You may even walk past a property that you like and decide to do a letterbox drop to see if the owner would be interested in selling.

Whatever the case, this is a time-consuming exercise and, unless you have a buyers agent working for you, you're better off focusing on your day job and using the Internet to locate potential deals.

Keep in mind that people who try to sell their property without the help of a selling agent usually hold out for a price far in excess of what the market is prepared to pay because they have an emotional attachment.

Research reports

Many companies claim to carry out research for the benefit of their clients. Property investment is one of the biggest investments you'll make in your life, so it's worth questioning the facts in the reports.

Was the report conducted by an independent body or was it commissioned by a company who may have an interest in the outcome of the report being positive?

If it's a company claiming to provide free advice, question whether that advice is sound or whether it's a sales pitch. The report may be highlighting benefits and ignoring risks.

Shortlisting from the armchair

Without a doubt, the most time consuming part of searching for a property is hitting the pavement and going to endless inspections. Consider researching the market from the comfort of your own home.

If you've worked through the exercises in this book, you'll know whether you are going for a high-yield or high-growth strategy; you've identified the criteria and know the level of risk you're comfortable with.

Armed with this knowledge, the most effective way of researching for property is with a top-down, area-based approach.

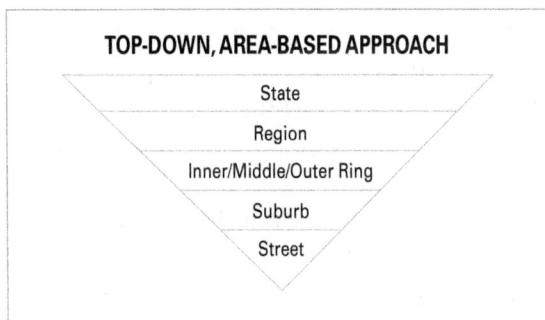

TOP-DOWN, AREA-BASED APPROACH

State

Region

Inner/Middle/Outer Ring

Suburb

Street

Now that you have a preference for specific areas or suburbs, you can then plug the criteria into an online search along with your budget to see what comes up.

Evaluate the properties that you find to see whether they match your risk profile, your strategy and your budget.

One of the most effective but little-known ways of refining this search is 'Show properties on map' – a link that can usually be found at the top of the results list from your online search.

The 'properties on map' view shows important data such as:

- checking location of shops and transport
- avoiding main roads
- avoiding industrial areas.

Online searches can also allow you to check property details such as lift access, whether it's a large or small complex, rates and strata levy fees.

Hitting the pavement

If you're looking to search for property without any professional help, the general rule amongst investors is that you need to see between 50 to 100 properties to have an understanding of the market. If you view five to 10 properties on a weekend, it should take up to three to four months before you know the market well.

More people are turning to a professional buyers agent who not only has seen thousands of properties but also has the skills to make sure you purchase the right property in your price range.

An advantage of going to inspections is that you get a real feel for the differences between properties such as:

- layout – does it work?
- light – is there enough natural light coming in?
- condition – will some rooms require renovation where others won't?

- aspect – are the views from the property pleasant?
- motivation – how keen are the vendors to sell?

Viewing properties also gives you an opportunity to discuss details of the property with the sales agent such as:

- strata fees
- price guide
- quantity (if unit block)
- rental estimate
- meterage (size m^2)

As you can see, much of this work can be done before you even leave home. Shopping for an investment property can be time consuming so aim for efficiency and gather as much information as you can from reputable sources before you get out there and hit the pavement. Stay focused on your search criteria, don't be lured by other potential deals in areas you're not familiar with and you'll be well on your way to a quick and successful deal.

DUE DILIGENCE

*The individual investor should
act consistently as an investor
and not as a speculator.*

Ben Graham

So you've selected a property that ticks most (or all) of your boxes and the feedback from the agent has told you that it's within your price range. So what now?

This is the time to inspect the property and make sure that you're getting what you are intending to pay for. If there are any impediments, this is the time to find out about them.

In the excitement (or tension) of buying property, many people overlook this process, choosing to either save their money or 'have a thorough look over things' themselves.

It seems strange that many are willing to pay hundreds of thousands of dollars for a property but are reluctant to spend a thousand dollars to make sure the property has no substantial issues before they make the purchase.

*It's wise to do due diligence on every property that you
are seriously considering. Think of it like an insurance
policy. It may cost a little up front but it could save you
years of wasted resources or unexpected expenses
down the line.*

The following items are considered due diligence. While some are compulsory, such as reviewing the contract by a conveyancer or solicitor, other inspections will be your responsibility.

Conveyancing

When you are serious about purchasing a property, you should ask for the contract from the selling agent so your conveyancer or solicitor can review the terms. This is a relatively simple process and, once reviewed, they will report back on anything you need to be aware of.

In reality, most contracts are quite standard and the important parts can be summarised in a short email from your solicitor or conveyancer. There's no need to look over their shoulder, but it pays to look for the following.

Inclusions

These are found on the front page of the contract and are ticked off if the items are included in the sale. This can be important to note. For example, if you thought the dishwasher was included in the sale but isn't in the inclusion list, it is best to find out why.

Settlement period

While the standard period is usually 42 days, double-check what is shown in the contract. Unless it's a cash sale, it can be quite difficult to settle the purchase in less than 30 days simply because lenders need time to process their paperwork.

If the vendor has selected a different period, ask why, as it can be a good point for negotiation. It may be that the owner needs time to move out or find a new place to live.

Release of deposit

This is a standard clause that is included in most conveyancing templates and allows the seller to take your deposit money straight away rather than waiting until settlement. Although this can be used as a point of negotiation, the difficulty comes if the sale falls through and the seller has spent the money elsewhere. The funds can then be quite difficult to get back. So while this clause is a standard inclusion for the seller, it is often deleted by the buyer.

Conveyancer or solicitor?

While the review of contracts has usually been in the solicitor's domain, the speed that some property transactions require and the relatively low cost of the service have led to the conveyancing arm of legal firms specialising in property contracts. This has led to a faster and more cost-effective option as the full breadth of expertise from the solicitor is simply not needed.

While it can be useful to have the expertise of a solicitor on hand if things get complicated, a conveyancer is usually more than sufficient for standard contracts and often far cheaper.

Apart from having the contract reviewed in a professional manner (which is expected), one of the most important aspects to look for from your conveyancer or solicitor is speed. Too many people have lost deals because they have had their family's solicitor look things over and it took them a week to get it back. Speed can be paramount to getting a deal across the line. Ask your conveyancer or solicitor to have the contract and information to you within a day or two or find someone else who can.

It's also wise to avoid minor changes like how much interest will be charged if one party (vendor or purchaser) delays settlement – often suggested by the solicitor trying to add some value for you. This penny-pinching negotiation can take far too much time going back and forth between parties. In the meantime, another buyer can come in and snatch the deal from under you. Make sure your intentions are known to your solicitor – keep superfluous changes to a minimum and focus on the bigger picture.

Independent valuations

It's important to engage the valuer before you make an offer.

Not to be confused with a bank valuation, which is when your lender verifies that the property is indeed worth what you are paying for it, an independent valuation is when you engage the valuer. That means you pay for them, so they work for you.

Even trained buying professionals such as buyers agents engage a valuer to verify the market value of every property before purchasing.

Many people hesitate at spending the money to engage a valuer on a property that they may not end up buying. At worst, you may find you have outlaid a few hundred dollars to have your own opinion verified. At best, you may find that the asking price is far above, or below, its real value. At least then you have the opportunity to walk away if the price is too high or grab it before anyone else realises what they have missed if the price is low.

Inspections

To ensure that the property you are buying has no defects or other costly issues, you can get some information from some inspections.

Building inspection

One of the most important items for due diligence, a building inspection, identifies structural issues, water problems, areas requiring maintenance, concrete cancer and other onerous issues.

While a building inspection makes a lot of sense when looking over a house, some doubt the value for an apartment purchase. However, a building inspection can often identify potential problems such as high-moisture content in walls which could be the source of a water leak, or concrete cancer on the balcony which can be part of a much larger issue.

Keep in mind that building inspection reports often paint the property in an unflattering light. Due to the liabilities that could arise from failing to identify issues, inspectors tend to take a 'glass half empty' approach to appearances and are more inclined to tell you that the place is falling down even though you think everything is fine.

One thing to remember with building inspections is that while the inspector can highlight the issues, they cannot suggest how the problem can be fixed or at what cost. This could lead to potential conflict where the inspectors may have a vested interest in identifying problems in order to create more work for themselves.

Pest inspection

Often the pest inspection is done together with the building inspection. These reports are most valuable when some structural part of the property is built in timber.

As apartment blocks are generally built using brick or concrete, a pest inspection is often not necessary for units. Units generally have issues with rodents and cockroaches which can usually be eradicated with baits and treatment.

While the pest inspector can identify problems with rodents and cockroaches, the main concerns will generally always be termites and/or borers. These little pests can compromise the whole structure.

While they can easily be treated, the main expense lies in the replacement of any timber work they may have destroyed or any preventative measures that need to be put in place to stop them coming back.

TOUCHING THE EARTH

While having contact with the earth may tend to ground us, it's not what we want when we're looking for property. Although untreated timber piers are not acceptable in building codes today, many older houses were built by putting timber piers directly into the earth. Put simply, this is termite-food. If they haven't made their way to this timber, it will only be a matter of time.

It's always best to inspect whether the house footings have ant caps (little covers to prevent ants crawling up the piers) and that they are built on brick or concrete piers. Alternatively, if there are structural piers used in the decks or other areas of the property, make sure that the timber is treated to prevent timber pests.

Strata report

If you are buying into an apartment block, the strata report is one of the most important documents (and cheapest) that you can buy.

As the name suggests, this is the review of the strata records that come with an apartment block. The document is an outline of any meetings the owners have had in the past three to five years, the financial records and spending of the owners' corporation and general discussions about maintenance, repairs and improvements.

While it's generally accepted that owners who also occupy the building will tend to look after the place better than tenants, it may not always be possible to find out this sort of information through an inspection.

A strata report is a good way to see whether the owners care about their asset. It is a measure of the health of the building, and, while it won't outline every activity that is going on between the owners, it will alert you to some of the most valuable points of conversation such as:

- disputes between owners, including legal issues

- any 'problem tenants' who have been brought to the owner's attention

- lack of proper management and general upkeep of the building

- lack of interest from other owners within the building

- any special levies that may be coming up in the near future.

This last point can be the single most valuable insight from the strata report. Disputes and disagreements are par for the course, but special levies can amount to tens of thousands of dollars for each owner to repair or improve the property at large – not the sort of bill you would like to receive just after you have bought your unit.

DOING YOUR DUE DILIGENCE

☐ Contract sent to conveyancer or solicitor for review

☐ Independent valuation ordered

☐ Building and/or pest inspection ordered

☐ Strata report ordered (if unit)

NEGOTIATION AND MAKING OFFERS

Care, but not too much.

Unknown

For those of us who rarely get involved in negotiations, the process of negotiation can be quite daunting, especially when up against professional sales agents who are trained to get the highest prices for their clients.

Most people will think that negotiation consists of one party looking for the lowest price, the other party looking for the highest price and the two meeting somewhere in the middle. While this one-dimensional, price-based outcome can be common, there is often a lot more to it than that.

Putting a deal together

There are a number of tools, apart from price, available to you that can make a deal more attractive for both parties. Often these tools are left as 'standard settings' and are never questioned, but they can often be the trade-off for a much lower (or higher) price.

This is not to say that these tools can be used in all negotiations. They may be appropriate in some cases but not in others. For example, you may be negotiating for a home and may be the only party in discussion with the seller. In this case, both parties may want the deal structured in a way that disrupts home life as little as possible. In other cases, a sought-after investment unit that may have 10 interested parties all looking to purchase may need a swift and convincing offer to take it off the market quickly.

Understanding which tools you have available and when to use them will give you the ability to create a deal where both parties walk away feeling like they got what they wanted.

Items to negotiate

While selling agents set prices for properties, there is always room to negotiate so that you get a better deal that will suit both you and the vendor.

Unconditional exchange

All states other than Tasmania and Western Australia have a 'cooling-off period' for non-auction purchases so that once an offer has been accepted the buyer has an opportunity to do their due diligence. This means that there are usually three to five days before the contract officially exchanges and the property contract is considered 'unconditionally exchanged'.

The disadvantage of a cooling-off period is that the buyer can pull out of the deal during this period. While this may not seem important to the buyer, if the buyer were to pull out of the deal after turning all other prospects away, the seller may lose all possibility of selling the property. Many sellers these days will request only unconditional contracts are submitted for this reason.

An unconditional exchange waives this cooling-off period so that the signed contract is exchanged immediately and the deal is done.

Offering an unconditional exchange, together with a full deposit of 10%, tells the seller that you're serious. It is one of the most convincing offers you can make. However, it's essential that due diligence is done prior to this offer as there is no turning back once the contract has been signed.

Lower deposit

The strongest position when it comes to a deposit is to offer 10% of the purchase price. In some cases, your cash flow may be tight and you may prefer a smaller deposit. A 5% deposit may be considered quite acceptable by the vendor if that's all you have to put down. Sometimes it's often simply a matter of asking.

It is possible to exchange on any amount of funds, even as low as a dollar, however, for standard residential purchases, offer anything less than 5% and the seller will probably doubt your capacity to purchase and may accept a lower price from another party that they're more confident will complete the transaction.

Release of deposit

Releasing the deposit allows the seller to use the deposit funds immediately upon exchange rather than having that money held in trust by the agent until the property has settled.

The danger in this release comes if the sale falls through and the buyer then needs the funds back. If the seller has put the funds towards another property, it can be very difficult to gain access to the deposit money.

Conversely, it can work in your favour to release the deposit to the seller because the seller needs the money to buy their next home. You may be able to negotiate a lower price because of this.

To avoid the risk of having to chase your money should the sale fall through, your solicitor or conveyancer will place a caveat over the property legally entitling you to make a financial claim to the property should events turn sour.

Settlement period

The time between when you exchange contracts and when you officially take ownership of the property is called the settlement period. This is 42 days in most cases and is usually determined by the time the lender needs to get their paperwork in order for the transfer of funds.

This can be a very useful negotiating tool depending on the seller's situation. If they're an investor, they may need to settle quickly so it can be useful to reduce the period to 30 days (this is the quickest it can usually be done). If the seller is an owner-occupier and they need to find a new place to live, they may need two months, three months or even six months. It all depends on what will work for them and that's where the value lies.

Tailoring a smooth exit for the seller can be so much more attractive to them than haggling over a few thousand dollars.

It can also work the other way, that is, timing when to take ownership to suit you. For example, if settlement on an investment property is the middle of winter, extending settlement for another eight weeks means that settlement will be in spring when the rental market is stronger and you have a better chance of getting a tenant.

Inclusions

Often overlooked by many buyers and sellers, the items that are to be included in the sale of the property can make all the difference when the negotiation comes down to the wire and each party is refusing to budge without a concession from the other.

Items such as custom curtains, high-end appliances, storage cupboards or integrated sound systems may not appear to be high value compared with the value of the property but they can save a lot of inconvenience for the purchaser down the track. For those who value their time, the thought of having to run around and replace all these items can break a deal or push it over the line in that final hour.

Repairs

Assuming you've done your due diligence and you are aware of any repairs and maintenance the property needs, it can be useful to use these as concessions for a trade-off. If the seller is asking for a higher price or a quick settlement, you could agree if they take care of some of the repairs that are needed to the property.

This may not amount to much, but it can save a lot of headache in dealing with tradesmen and could mean having a tenant in the property a week or two earlier. The inspection prior to settlement is needed to make sure the repairs have been completed satisfactorily.

Early tenancy

Early tenancy works when the property becomes vacant over the settlement period and it's possible to get a tenant straight away. This can work well for you as an investor by reducing any downtime in finding a tenant.

Technically, the property still belongs to the seller, however, if they're flexible and willing, it can work for both parties to have a tenant move in as the seller collects the rent up until the point of settlement and the buyer has the advantage of having a tenant from day one.

For a smooth execution, it's helpful to have a rental property manager prepare two tenancy agreements and they also need to allay any fears that the seller may have over the short term.

Early access

Early access allows the buyer to enter the property prior to the settlement date to begin renovation or building work. This can be difficult to get agreement as the property still belongs to the seller and, if the sale were to fall through, they would be left with a property that is only half renovated.

Adding terms that, if the sale falls through, the property will be reverted to its original condition, can reduce such fears.

The benefit for the buyer is that, by the time they own the property, they could have completed mostly, if not all, the improvements to the property. This can make a massive difference to the period in which the property may sit empty without tenants. For those looking to 'flip' the property and on-sell, it can dramatically reduce the holding costs of the property before it moves to the next owner.

Mastering the negotiation

While it's important to know what tools you have available to use in a negotiation, if you can't get on with the other party, it won't matter what you're after, you most likely won't get it.

Many people who aren't used to property negotiations overestimate their position, believing that going in hard or having a 'take it or leave it' attitude is the way to get what they want. In reality, they often create an enemy of the other party or get pushed aside by a number of other people who are willing to make it work with less fuss and a little more flexibility.

The skills of negotiation

Understanding how to work together to achieve an outcome that works for both you and the seller is one of the most valuable skills you can have.

Rather than come from the traditional stance that a negotiation is a battle, where one party wins and the other loses, the following techniques are designed to provide a win/win scenario where both parties walk away feeling like they got what they wanted.

Creating a third position

It's important to remember that a negotiation is an exchange of energy. Place two people face to face and they will feel confronted. Pride, stubbornness and ego can get in the way because each person feels they're being threatened personally.

Creating a third position, where both people turn to face the problem, diverts the intense energy of each person away from confrontation and focuses their attention on solving the issue.

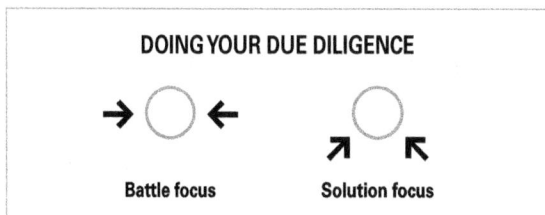

DOING YOUR DUE DILIGENCE

Battle focus   **Solution focus**

Separating the problem from the person avoids any personality clashes and reduces the chance of offending the other person. Rather than reacting harshly to the other party not wanting to drop their price because they're 'stubborn and unreasonable', you can instead focus attention on the problem. Take personality out of the equation and focus on finding a solution rather than becoming defensive and equally unreasonable.

Look for the 'why?'

Most people will make a decision based on reason. Finding out what that reason is can be an invaluable strategy as it gives you the opportunity to create a solution, often in return for what you want.

For example, if the seller must have an extended settlement of three months due to the timing of another property they bought, they may accept a lower price or a smaller deposit. They're left with a more convenient time to move while you can make savings on the purchase price or interest repayments.

Avoid getting personal

No one likes to be attacked personally. Even when you're negotiating through the selling agent, you have to assume that the agent may communicate your every word to the seller. So keep it polite and remember that you're trying to get them to cooperate.

Blaming the other party or reacting to them negatively can work against your goals. Even when something doesn't go your way, you may well sacrifice a long-term gain, such as purchasing a great property, because the seller wouldn't throw in the dishwasher.

You also need to avoid thinking the worst of the other party. Just because they request that the deposit be released doesn't mean they're going to steal your money. This can be difficult as you don't know who you're dealing with in a property transaction. However, assuming the worst of the other person will rarely be productive. Remember, they may actually be thinking the same about you.

Be flexible

The more flexible you can be towards the other party, the more likely they will be willing to give you what you want.

If you can decide what you want before you go into the negotiation, such as your top price, settlement terms or minimum deposit, you can often give the seller what they want without having to sacrifice your position.

Think of the other person

At the end of the day, a negotiation, however brief, is a relationship. If you fail to consider the other person's feelings or what they want then it is unlikely you will have much success.

If they are resolute about particular items – price, terms, inclusions – it can be beneficial to withhold your judgment and put yourself in their shoes. Is there a reason why they're being so firm? Is there something important to them that you haven't considered? After all, you may very well do the same thing if you were in their position.

Having some empathy for the other person can often ease the pressure enough to get them across the line on other things, such as selling to you rather than the next person.

Using 'if'

One of the secrets to a successful negotiation is to never give anything up without asking for something in return, even if it's small. Using 'if' through your negotiation is a good way to handle this.

If I give you ... then I would like ...

I'm happy to give you ... if ...

If you can ... then I'd be more than happy to ...

Use silence

One of the most effective ways to negotiate is to stay quiet. This may not be appropriate in situations where there are five other buyers wanting the same property, but it can be invaluable when the seller is poised on a favourable outcome.

While this can sometimes be accidental, staying silent can communicate a lack of interest, causing the seller to second-guess your position. Having the 'ball in your court', so to speak, leaves you with the power to make the next call. In the meantime, the seller waits in anticipation, hoping that they may achieve their outcome. This can create the impression for the seller that the selling process may soon end with a good result and they can walk away happy. When you do come back to the table with a counter offer, the seller's anticipation of closing the deal soon can often make the seller more willing to sacrifice items that they may have fought hard to get earlier, all because they've seen the light at the end of the tunnel.

Silence can be useful for difficult negotiations as it can give the time needed for both parties to 'cool off'. Sitting back can give you the perspective you need to get a better understanding of the situation and provide you with the long-term view that you need.

Dealing with sales agents

There's no doubt that real estate agents have a reputation that is not necessarily favourable. The property market can involve a lot of money and a lot of emotion.

Be open

If you meet an agent at an open for inspection, it pays to engage with them. They have properties to sell and you're looking for something to buy so it's best to let them know what you're looking for. Remember, if you don't ask, you won't get.

Be friendly and respectful

Agents are people too, so strike up a conversation and keep it friendly. You never know when you might come across them again and a bad relationship will do you no favours when it comes to negotiation time.

Let them know you're serious

One of the biggest time commitments for an agent is sorting the serious buyers from the 'tyre kickers'. You will have more traction with an agent if they know you're ready to buy and can transact quickly. It helps to let them know that you're pre-approved for finance and looking to buy immediately. Needless to say, if you're not pre-approved or ready to buy, you shouldn't be saying these things.

Get back to them

If an agent calls you to enquire about what you thought of a property, it's because they're doing their job and you may want some more information. If they leave a message, it's best to pay them the respect of getting back to them and letting them know your interest one way or the other. Remember, these are the people who may very well place the deal of the year in your lap.

Keep a respectful distance

Although the above points are valid, it's important to remember that the sales agents do not work for you. They are paid by the vendor, the person selling the property, and it is their job to get the best deal for their client. This point can't be stressed enough. By all means build a relationship, but keep a professional distance.

When to make offers

The two ways in which a property can be sold:

- by private treaty

- at auction.

Private treaty

If a property is being sold as private treaty then the price will be advertised and you have the chance to negotiate on that price. There is no official time frame in which the vendor can accept offers. Basically, if you were to give them their asking price, they would sell immediately.

However, if you want to negotiate at a lower price, have all your finance in order and your due diligence ready to go so that you can make an offer and close the deal quickly. Low offers tend to attract other potential buyers who get wind of a bargain and can push up the price.

Offers at auction

Auction campaigns have a set time frame and it is usually expected that the vendor will be selling on auction day if they achieve the price they want – unless they decide to accept an offer prior.

While auction campaigns usually run for four weeks, from an agent's perspective they run for six. This is because any property that doesn't sell on the big day usually has a two-week window to attract any latecomers before the market loses interest and it becomes very difficult to sell.

Looking at it from this perspective, the auction is made up of three parts – pre-auction, auction day and post auction.

Auctions are popular because they can attract a higher price on auction day. Normally rational, level-headed people can be whipped into an emotional buying frenzy when all placed in a room on auction day.

However, with higher reward comes higher risk and there's always the chance that the auction doesn't reach the 'reserve price'. After having people walk through their property for four weeks, the notion of not selling can be quite unattractive to a vendor. As a result, it is not uncommon for vendors to sell prior to auction. These are the types of properties that can be the most attractive – the properties are popular enough to create an auction campaign. However, the vendors are also willing to sell for a fair price rather than risk not selling at auction.

Making a successful pre-auction offer

Securing a property before it goes to auction can be one of the most successful strategies you can undertake as a buyer looking to secure a quality property. However, it is not without its pitfalls and understanding the timing can be key to success.

Needless to say, the first thing you should be asking the selling agent is whether the vendor is willing to sell prior to auction. The agent should tell you straight away so you can avoid wasting time on due diligence only to find that the vendor is insisting on going to auction.

Week 1

Provided you see the property before it goes to market or on the first weekend, you can usually afford one week to conduct due diligence. Making an offer in this first week can often be premature as the vendor still has three weeks left until the auction date and no clear signal from the market as to what buyers think of the property – whether it's hot or not.

If the economy or the market is showing some signs of weakness, it can be in the vendor's interests to take a fair market offer prior to auction day (a bird in the hand).

Sometimes the vendor's situation can play a part too. A family death or divorce can mean the vendors would rather sell at a fair price and move on rather than wait for that incremental bonus that may be achieved at auction.

Week 2

Once the campaign has moved into the second week, the seller has normally had two open for inspections and is often keen to get a gauge from the agent how the market is reacting.

This is typically the best time to make an offer. If the seller is getting price feedback at a certain level and your due diligence shows that the price is indeed fair, it can be worth your while to offer that price rather than take the risk that it could go to auction and be lost to an emotional buyer who ends up paying far more on the day.

Remember, this tactic is not about 'bagging a bargain'. It's a far more powerful strategy to get the right property in your portfolio that will have strong growth year on year rather than grabbing a bargain that underperforms or goes nowhere for the next 10 years.

Weeks 3 and 4

If the market is reacting favourably to the property, then the chance of securing the property prior to auction day diminishes as the campaign moves into weeks 3 and 4. The vendor is into the second half of the campaign and, if there has been strong interest in the property, at this stage, they would rather take their chances on the day and see what happens.

Few properties will sell in the final week prior to the actual auction day. For those properties that do sell, the vendor may feel that the price they were hoping for has been reached and to try to push for a higher figure could result in losing the buyer altogether. After all, the auction holds no guarantee of a sale and not every buyer will want to go to auction. In this case, a bird in the hand is more valuable.

Weeks 5 and 6 – post-auction

If the property passes in (doesn't sell at auction), but has had enthusiastic bidders, it is likely that the vendor can reach an agreement immediately following the auction. Vendor greed or unrealistic expectations are usually the cause of properties not selling on auction day and this often results in the property being placed back on to the market at an undisclosed price.

If the auction moves into the fifth and sixth week, power shifts from the seller to the buyer. The seller obviously wanted to sell and failed to do so on the big day and now interest from buyers can quickly start to fade if not handled properly.

For those buyers who were genuine, the motivation of the vendor to sell is now in question and immediately puts doubt into buyers' minds that the vendor may not sell at all. As a result, where once the buyers were knocking down their door to get the property at auction, now they're walking off into the sunset. The heat can come out of the market very quickly and many buyers, believing they can't afford the property, become disinterested and start looking elsewhere.

The remaining buyers sense an opportunity to take advantage of the vendor's anxiety and start making lower offers. If the property has emotional appeal and the selling agent knows the market, it's often wise for the vendor to hold out for their price as the tension often forces a motivated buyer who may have fallen in love with the property to revisit their finances to find the extra funds.

In many cases, the market simply loses interest. Suddenly the seller is forced to drop their price. Where once they would have had buyers swarming to buy at a higher price level, now they're left with nothing but an occasional enquiry.

It goes without saying that this can be an excellent time to pick up a quality property. The market has moved on, the seller has dropped their price and, knowing the true value of the property, you are ready to take advantage of the reduced price. You can move forward with tough negotiations knowing that the seller has few options but to take your offer and move on.

Verbal vs. written offers

Most of the time a verbal offer is not worth the paper it's not written on. A written offer is far more powerful. It's money on the table and it tells the selling party that you're serious and that you're here to do a deal.

Often buyers think that they will 'test the waters' with a verbal offer. In some cases, where there are no other interested parties to fend off, they may have time to negotiate a variety of terms to suit both the vendor and themselves before anyone else arrives to spoil the party.

However, do not mistake this situation for a smoking hot property that is pulling in 30 groups on a weekend. In these cases, the vendor and selling agent hold the cards and, if you want to play at the table, you had better come forward with a serious written offer or risk getting bowled over in the mad rush that's following behind.

What's a serious offer? In this game, words are cheap and a signed, unconditional contract with a 10% deposit is the only way to get attention. In order to have this in place you need to be prepared – you need to be sure that your due diligence has checked out and that your finances are in order (the first step in the process).

This is not the time for low-ball offers either. If you've been communicating with the agent and your valuation is in the ballpark of the seller, expectations then you know what the property is worth. Pay the money and take the trophy home.

If you would like to take a nibble at a lower price first, hoping to save yourself ten or twenty thousand dollars or more, consider this – once the agent has received your less-than-expected offer they have a 'duty to inform all other contract holders' that an offer is now on the table. The agent won't normally tell people what the offer is, but they can insinuate what it might be and it is their job to prompt the prospective buyers to 'put their best foot forward'. This is not a good situation.

Those buyers who were dragging their feet suddenly snap to attention and within 24 hours have bowled over your low-ball offer with an emotionally-charged price that is motivated by the fear of missing out. Your hope of securing this property at any reasonable price has now flown out the window.

Had you offered a fair price, one that was in line with expectations, the selling agent would have more than likely approached their vendor with the 'bird in the hand' offer and you may have secured the property for a price that was reasonable and worthy of mentioning at the next dinner party.

FINAL WORDS

My motivation to write this book has always been about creating wealth and personal empowerment. I've always imagined that these provide the greatest freedom – to be free from the financial constraints that are so often present in our daily lives and to be endowed with the knowledge and wisdom that it took to create our wealth – a truly sustainable position.

The road to personal wealth takes dedication and commitment and it's essential that we start with the end in mind.

My partner Julie and I have done this quite literally and I sit daily at my desk with my vision board in front of me. This is my leisure bucket and I'm reminded every day of what it's all for. For those of you who need some inspiration, you can visit my Pinterest site (in Contact information) and check out my 'Time to start living' board.

If you've read this far then you will also understand that property investment can be a truly powerful tool in an investment portfolio. Like anything, the key is to start small and keep it simple. No need to get involved in convoluted strategies.

- Work out where you are today.

- Tailor your strategy to fit.

- Apply the tactics to maximise your returns.

- As soon as practically possible, repeat.

That's it. Often the hardest thing to do is to keep things simple.

So let's look at what has been covered in this book.

It all starts with mindset   Make a plan, keep it simple, be proactive and stay in it for the long term. Having a calm and calculating mind to weather the ups and downs will make all the difference when it comes to playing against those who simply react to what's in front of them.

Get your head around the numbers   Don't be daunted by debt levels. The numbers might seem large but a well-bought property shouldn't cost more than 1.5% to 2% of the total cost every year. Some may cost far less. The key is to let the investment mature over time and in the end you will walk away with much more than it cost to maintain.

Pick your strategy   Growth or yield – you can't have both. High-yield strategies are great for those on lower incomes who need the financial support to hold as well as diversify. These properties provide income that goes straight to the bottom line. However, lower asset growth means it can be difficult to gather enough steam for the next deposit.

High-growth investors who can afford to sacrifice a small amount of income each year can surge ahead and find themselves awash with equity to use as a deposit for the next investment.

The best of both worlds is hard to find, so make sure you know which path you need to take to meet the goals you've set for yourself.

**Maximise
your return**

Like any asset, property prices are based on supply and demand. Invest where there is strong demand with a stable population and strong job centres. Also make sure that there is limited supply within the area. If people can get only so much of a good thing, prices are bound to go up.

Invest in an area and property that people will want to live in, so look for light, space and convenience and try and keep those maintenance costs as low as possible.

Investing is also about minimising risk. Keep an eye on the prize, but don't forget to weigh up the costs. Look at the population, watch your price point and cast a keen eye over the property itself and you will have a much better chance of reducing any potential losses for the future.

Equity is king

Very few of us have the ability to save a 10% to 20% deposit each time we want to buy a property. The key to building a portfolio lies in being able to access our equity to leverage into the next property, and the next, without having to break into a sweat to do so. Build equity, draw down and use your newly formed funds to reinvest into your next great venture.

**Build a
quality team**

Property investing is a team sport. Your team will be there to help get your finances in order, ensure you're getting what you paid for, deal with the legal jargon and manage the investment once you own it. They will be the most critical part of your success so choose them wisely and treat them well.

I truly hope the information you've found within this book has been useful. It has come from years of working in the business, building my own property portfolio, and working as a buyers agent to help others build theirs.

If you would like to reach me personally to ask me questions, feel free to reach me via one of my social media sites. I'd love your feedback.

Finally, I hope this has given you the spark that you need to help you move forward on the next journey of your life – to build a better future that really is a life worth living.

Remember, the time to start building your wealth with property is now.

GLOSSARY

appreciating asset   an asset that continues to grow in value over time, for example, property

ICCA   Institute of Chartered Accountants Australia

Capital Gains Tax (CGT)   applies to the capital gain made on disposal of any asset, except for specific exemptions

caveat   is a legal entitlement to make a financial claim to the property, from Latin, literally 'let a person beware'

compound growth   is when the profits from an investment are reinvested to increase your wealth

CPA   Certified Public Accountants

depreciating asset   falls in value over time, for example a car

evocities   so called because they are centres of **e**nergy, **v**ision and **o**pportunity – regional NSW centres are Albury, Bathurst, Dubbo, Orange, Tamworth and Wagga Wagga

gazumping   can happen during the cooling-off period before the contract of sale is 'exchanged' when the vendor accepts a higher offer or the purchaser pulls out of the contract

GFC   global financial crisis

inflation   the amount that prices rise each year compared to the last

IPO	an initial public offering or stock market launch is a type of public offering where shares of stock in a company are sold to the general public, on a securities exchange, for the first time
leaseback	is an arrangement in which one party sells a property to a buyer and the buyer immediately leases the property back to the seller – allows the initial buyer to make full use of the asset while not having capital tied up in the asset – can sometimes provide tax benefits
lender's mortgage insurance (LMI)	insurance that the lender requests from the purchaser against any default to pay a mortgage
leverage	the ability to multiply your investment efforts with a relatively small outlay
line of credit (LOC)	an arrangement between a financial institution and a customer to establishe the maximum borrowing that the customer can draw down
Loan to Valuation Ratio (LVR)	the percentage that a lender is willing to lend
margin call	having to sell an asset (shares) to avoid further losses when the price falls below the purchase price
options	the right but not the obligation to purchase an asset at a particular time and price in the future
principal and interest (P&I) loan	when you borrow money to buy something then pay the money back that you borrowed over time plus the interest – and then you own it

interest only (IO) loan   when you only pay the interest owing on a loan and none of the principal amount borrowed

principal place of residence (PPOR)   where you live – this property is different to your investment properties and as your place of residence is exempt from capital gains tax when you sell

reserve price   the preset price for an auction that the vendor will take at auction

settlement period   the time between the exchange of contracts and the actual purchase when the buyer takes ownership of the property – usually about 42 days to give time for legal matters to be completed

tyre kickers   industry term for people who attend open for inspections for a look – not genuine buyers

wrap   is a technique that permits an existing loan to be refinanced at an interest rate between the original loan rate and the currently prevailing market rate

INDEX

ABOUT THE AUTHOR

Josh gained a Bachelor of Business at the University of Technology Sydney in 1994 and spent much of his early career in hospitality, working in restaurants in Sydney, London and Vancouver.

In 2002 he went on to become the owner operator of a restaurant on the New South Wales north coast near Byron Bay before selling up 2004 and returning to Sydney to pursue a more creative career in interior design.

Josh studied at Enmore Design College before moving on to work for COMA, a interior retail fit-out group, and then Palazzo Design Group, specializing in custom furniture design and architectural fit-outs inspired by Versace.

Josh then went on to open his own interior design studio, working throughout Sydney doing residential interior fit-outs, development applications and design work.

After being involved in a number of successful property transactions through the studio in 2010, Josh decided to pursue property purchasing full-time, effectively closing the design studio to co-ordinate deals with agents and pursue joint venture partners.

Josh now works full-time as a Buyer's Agent and is the director of BuySide, a Sydney based Buyers Agency that specialises in locating and securing investment properties for clients in both the Sydney and Brisbane markets.

Josh has contributed to the Switzer Super Report and has also featured on Sky Business News. He has also has recently released Suburb Investor, a mobile app to help property investors compare growth rates for any suburb across Australia.

Josh currently lives on Sydney's eastern beaches with his wife Julie and dog Molly.

CONTACT INFORMATION

For more information about buying for your first investment property or building your property portfolio, please email josh@buyside.com.au

Want to connect more often?

Become part of the 7000+ facebook fans and get daily updates and inspiration to help you on your journey.

facebook.com/buyingproperty

twitter.com/joshmasters

linkedin.com/in/joshuamasters

pinterest.com/joshmasters

plus.google.com/+JoshMasters